Growing a Peaceful Heart

Growing a Peaceful Heart

Devotions of Faith, Encouragement,
and Forgiveness from Peacemakers
PAST, PRESENT, AND FUTURE

Karen Whiting & Sara DuBose

AMG
PUBLISHERS

Growing a Peaceful Heart:
Devotions of Faith, Encouragement, and Forgiveness,
from Peacemakers Past, Present, and Future

Copyright © 2022 by Karen Whiting & Sara DuBose

Published by AMG Publishers
6815 Shallowford Road
Chattanooga, Tennessee 37421

ISBN 13: 978-1-61715-578-9 Paper Back   978-1-61715-580-2 Mobi
978-1-61715- 579-6 EPub   978-1-61715-581-9 PDF

First Printing—September 2022

Cover designed by Jonathan Lewis, Jonlin Creative, Pekin, IL
Manuscript editing by Marissa Wold Uhrina, Eden Prairie, MN
Text design and layout by PerfecType, Nashville, TN

Printed in the United States of America

Dedicated to the memory of my father, John Hartigan, and my husband, James Whiting, two of the kindest people I ever knew. These men always strove for peace at home, in the community, and at work and served their country to bring world peace.

—Karen Whiting

To God, the author of peace and my Savior, and to my beloved husband, Bill, who models God's love and peace every day.

—Sara DuBose

TABLE OF CONTENTS

WEEK   **Personal Peace**

1. Peace with God   2
2. Inner Peace   12
3. Peace with the Past, Present, and Future   22
4. Havens of Peace   32
5. Emotional Peace   42
6. Peace in Grief and Loss   52
7. Peace with Letting Go of Control   62
8. Peace through Gratitude   72
9. Peace Reactions to Struggles and Strife   82
10. Peace and Rest   92
11. Blessed with Peace   102

Peace in Relationships

12. Peace with Mindfulness and Joy   112
13. Peace through Forgiveness and Acceptance   122
14. Peace in Relationships   132
15. Peace in the Home   142
16. Peace through Unity and Purpose   152
17. Peace through Kindness   162

18. Peace through Conflict Resolution   172

19. Peaceful Debates   182

20. Peace with the Past   192

21. Peace with Money   202

22. Peace and Compassion with Grace   212

23. Getting along with Others through Personalities 222

24. Peace with Gentleness and Humility   232

Becoming Peacemakers

25. Peace with the Community and World   242

26. Seeking Peace   252

27. Peace after War   262

28. Peace with Respect   272

29. Peacemakers   282

30. Praying for World Peace   292

PERSONAL PEACE

A great many people are trying to make peace, but that has already been done. God has not left it for us to do; all we have to do is to enter into it. —Dwight L. Moody

The word for peace in the Bible means to tie together into wholeness. It's being whole in mind, body, and soul. Jesus offers us peace when we ask, and we willingly let go of what keeps our minds and hearts from experiencing peace. This brings wholeness.

Week 1

Peace with God

Prayer for Peace that Passes Understanding

Father in heaven, I thank you for the gift of peace. I want a peace that lasts, a peace that only you can give. My days get busy, and news of trouble invades my world. Help me to not worry but trust that you are in control.

May I have an ever-growing understanding and appreciation for all you do. May I pause and remember all the blessings you have sent. May I also understand what you, Jesus, have done for me.

Lord, please forgive me when I wander from you and become self-absorbed. I ask you to help me be sorry when I hurt someone and to forgive me. Help me to let go of hurts and forgive those who cause me pain.

Help me learn to love and serve you with my whole heart! The more I learn about you and read your words of love, the more it brings me peace, the peace you promise that the world does not understand.

Wisdom from Young Peacemakers

I go outside and climb a tree to have peace.

When asked, what is peace, child answered: [Piece is] *Can I have a piece of cake, please?*

A Park Surprise

We have come to know and have believed the love which God has for us. God is love, and the one who remains in love remains in God, and God remains in him. 1 JOHN 4:16

"Mama, please. Could we go to the park?"

"Sure, why not?" Sara answered her eight- and ten-year-old daughters, DeAnn and Cherie. She loved to wander under the giant oaks and hickories.

Located in Montgomery, Alabama, Oak Park is a tranquil area. It's a place to think, play, and allow your soul beauty soaks. Sara packed some snacks, and they left.

Soon DeAnn and Cherie shared with Sara about where to stop: a place near their favorite swings and climbing bars. Sara sat on a bench admiring her two acrobats.

A young boy about nine ran and joined in the fun. They began with the usual "you do your thing and I'll do mine" action, but then they took turns pushing each other and playing tag.

Sara didn't catch any of their conversation, but they appeared to be enjoying themselves. Sara read the book she brought.

"Mama," DeAnn called, "will you come down a minute?"

Sighing, Sara slipped the book into her purse and walked over. Each child held a long stick and DeAnn pointed to a message scribbled in the sand. In large letters it read: "I can't hear or talk, but my name is DAN."

Under DAN, the girls had carefully written their names. The children looked serious as Dan held his branch to Sara. Sara wrote MOM under their names. A smile emerged from Dan's face—a smile that seemed to come from deep inside. Sara saw room for one more name. She took Dan's stick and wrote GOD, pointing up to the sky.

Dan's smile widened. Nodding, he pointed heavenward and to his heart. Dan took the stick and drew a circle around their names and then got up to touch each person.

> **Today's Peace Step**
> Look for opportunities to see God and share Him with others.

Four people—all children, really—and all in the circle of a caring God. Sara thanked God for their day of adventure and discovery.

Einstein Insight (Historic Story)

For by grace you have been saved through faith; and this is not of yourselves, it is the gift of God; not as a result of works, so that no one may boast. EPHESIANS 2:8–9

Brilliant scientist? Yes. Discoverer of the theory of relativity? Yes. Forgetful individual? Yes. How so?

Well, according to a little-known story, Einstein once boarded a train and was sorting his luggage when the conductor passed through the car to collect tickets.

"Hold on," Einstein said. "It's right here in my coat."

Einstein fumbled in two pockets and shook his head.

"That's odd," he mumbled. "I thought it was . . ."

"Never mind, Dr. Einstein," the conductor assured. "I know who you are. It's all right."

"But I need . . ."

"It's no problem. Believe me. I'm sure you purchased a ticket, sir."

As the conductor walked away Einstein reached up to retrieve a piece of luggage. While other passengers relaxed and chatted, Einstein continued his search, shuffling through papers, ties, shirts, a toothbrush, and even tools and test tubes.

Soon the conductor had collected everyone's tickets and passed Einstein for the third time. Frustrated and a bit annoyed, he gently chastised the famous scientist again, but Einstein replied, "You don't understand. I need to find the ticket because I don't know where I'm going."

> **Today's Peace Step**
>
> For inner peace, remind yourself of where you are going and who provided the way, and stay in contact with Jesus daily.

Most of us are not brilliant scientists, nor have we made any remarkable discoveries. However, we can all be forgetful. One thing to never forget is our ultimate destination. No ticket needed. We cannot buy salvation or earn our way to heaven. Jesus provided the ticket for us.

Scripture reminds us that that no one can boast. Our role is simply to follow Jesus!

I'm Here!

Truly, truly, I say to you, the one who hears My word, and believes Him who sent Me, has eternal life, and does not come into judgment, but has passed out of death into life. JOHN 5:24

Seven-year-old Johnny Brooks (name changed) was positive of his salvation. As devout Christians, his parents tried to make sure all of their children understood the gospel. One day they asked Johnny to share a bit about his faith, and he said something like this:

"Well, one day when we are in heaven an angel may call out to us and say, 'Daddy Brooks?' and Daddy will say, 'Here.' Then he will call, 'Mommy Brooks?' and Mommy will say, 'Here.' Next he will call my sisters, and they will say, 'Here.'"

Johnny paused, took a deep breath, and then added, "Finally, the angel will call my name. Now I'm kinda small, so maybe I'll need to call out real loud, 'I'm here!'"

A tragic accident occurred a few days after this event. As Johnny made his way to catch the school bus a car stuck him. Rushed by ambulance to the nearest hospital, all of the family gathered around Johnny's bedside. It wasn't long before doctors indicated there was little, or no, hope for his recovery.

The family waited and prayed. Late into the night Johnny seemed to stir, so the family drew closer. Then they watched as his lips moved. Just one phrase was uttered, and yet this phrase was profound. Yes, it was a phrase that would bring comfort to them for years to come. In a loud and clear voice, loud and clear enough for all to hear and understand, Johnny pronounced:

> **Today's Peace Step**
> Ask your loved ones to share about their faith so you will have the comfort of knowing they are believers.

"I'm here!"

His two words revealed that Johnny heard the voice and knew how to reply. Saying goodbye to his earthy family, Johnny was welcomed home!

True Peace (Biblical Story)

Behold, I am with you and will keep you wherever you go . . .
GENESIS *28:15*

Jesus told a story, in Luke 15, about a father of two sons. One son was selfish and asked his father to give him his share of the dad's estate. He had a "me first" attitude and quickly packed his stuff and left home. Once there, he wasted his life with wild living and spending. Soon a famine came, and the son had no more funds and no place to go. He hired himself out to feed pigs.

The second son made different choices. He had stayed home and stayed faithful to the family. However, this son was prideful, and when his brother came home and repented and their father royally accepted him back into the family, this guy became jealous.

What we need to notice here is how the father reached out to both sons. When the runaway returned he offered him love, peace, and forgiveness. When the jealous and prideful son rebelled, he reminded him of the love, peace, and acceptance he had always known in their household.

Sometimes we are like the first son: selfish and self-centered. Other times we react more like the second son. We think we have it all together. We would never run from

God, and we tend to think more highly of ourselves and snub others.

We see so much of our God's heart in this story. We may ignore, rebel, and flee from God like the first son, but when we repent, He is there. Or we may think we are right beside the Father and not see how far away we

> **Today's Peace Step**
> Be quick to confess any sin and rebellion today and be reminded of God's warm embrace and love for you.

really are. In both cases our God is the same. He comes to us with His out-stretched arms of peace. In fact, God sees us when we are still a long way off and runs to greet us. His peace is almost beyond understanding!

Good News

For God so loved the world, that He gave His only Son, so that everyone who believes in Him will not perish, but have eternal life. JOHN 3:16

What was that look on her three-year-old's face? Yes, she was approaching boredom.

"Cherie, are you okay?" Sara asked.

"Yes, Mama. I jest don't know what to do." She flailed her arms and shook her head.

"Is there a toy you haven't played with lately?"

The words were barely out of her mother's mouth when the light bulb turned on and Cherie said, "I be right back." Sara soon heard Cherie shoving toys in search of something.

Sara continued sweeping the kitchen floor and tried to imagine her daughter on her knees over the toy box as the rattling and bumping noises continued.

Several minutes later Cherie reappeared with a plastic megaphone and began her rant. "Dare are fires in California, storms in New York, and lots of fighting in the Mideast!"

Sara shook her head and responded, "Cherie, why don't you tell us some good news?"

"Mama," Cherie corrected. "You know dare ain't no good news!"

Although this story remains clear after many years, Sara's thoughts drift to something far better. She remembers a small flat rock. Why? Well, about one year later Cherie wrote a message of good news on that rock: I love God. Sara still treasures that rock with good news on it.

In addition to this, Sara can also look across the den to a small rocking chair. Today it houses a teddy bear, but one day when Cherie was about seven she recalls sitting in that chair when she suddenly had a fuller understanding of God. Now that is good news!

Today's Peace Step

Keep your focus on the good news of being forgiven for your sins and being a member of God's family rather than on negative news around you.

Week 2

Inner Peace

Prayer for Inner Peace

Dear Lord, you are the Prince of Peace. Remind me to not let my heart be troubled. News of battles and disasters or illness can be scary. Joyful words from loved ones and your Word lift me up again and I remember to trust in you. Help me dwell on my joys and pray over my struggles and hardships while trusting the outcomes to you.

While I look at one falling leaf, you see the whole forest and the seasons. You know the outcomes and remind me that you will take care of me, so I have only to focus on what you call me to do.

Calm my heart as I dwell on what is good and worthy. Let me count my blessings each morning and evening to remind me how much you care for me. When I face inner turmoil, help me still my heart and handle the situation with peace of mind and heart. Those are times for me to be still and know that you are God and in control. Thanks for being with me always.

Wisdom from Young Peacemakers

I pet the cat until it purrs.

I start thinking about things I love.

Predelivery Worries

The steadfast of mind You will keep in perfect peace because he trusts in You. ISAIAH 26:3

I don't want a c-section, Karen thought. Her third baby lay inside her in breach position with little chance of moving. Her babies came out so easy, with almost no labor.

That night her husband smiled and said, "Our baby is in God's hands." He prayed, and then drifted off to sleep.

Karen couldn't sleep. She knelt and cried out to God to turn the baby or give her peace. She read Scriptures and continued praying for hours, grappling with her thoughts and worries. At last, she felt inner peace. Back in bed, she felt the baby move one-quarter of the way around the womb. She smiled, thanked God, and said, "Lord, I'm okay no matter what happens."

Over the next few hours, the baby moved three quarters of the way around a circle. That placed the head in the right position. She saw the doctor a few days later.

He said, "You're beaming. The baby must have moved." Karen nodded.

> **Today's Peace Step**
> Pray for inner peace, no matter what the problem.

She described what happened. The doctor took notes and said, "Great position now."

When it came time to deliver the baby, the doctor said, "Take it easy. We need the baby to come out slowly."

Karen pushed, looked up, and listened as a nurse said, "Don't move." Her tone alarmed Karen.

Karen stretched her head and saw the cord around her baby's head. Her mentally disabled brother had choked on the umbilical cord at birth and that caused a lack of oxygen to his brain, so she understood the danger.

She held her breath as they cut the cord. Her son James slid out, perfectly healthy, although a bit jaundiced. She felt so relieved to hold her son. James, a genius, became a very kind and gentle rocket scientist. Years later James met the doctor who delivered him.

Hannah's Inner Turmoil (Biblical Story)

She [Hannah] said, "Let your bond-servant find favor in your sight." So the woman went on her way and ate, and her face was no longer sad. 1 SAMUEL 1:18

Tears flowed as Hannah prayed. Peninnah, the other wife of Hannah's husband, teased her continually because she had no children. Hannah wanted a baby of her own to hold and cuddle. She felt tired of Peninnah's verbal abuse. Her husband tried to comfort her because he loved her so much, but his words did not ease her longing. She could not eat because of the turmoil within her. Their husband gave them portions when he sacrificed but gave Hannah a double portion. That he favored Hannah probably hurt Peninnah and provoked her to tease Hannah more every year as they journeyed to Shiloh to worship. Two wives and contention probably caused plenty of tension in the home.

Hannah went in the temple to pray and even promised God that if He gave her a son, she would give that son back to Him to serve in the temple. She'd let go of the child she so dearly wanted.

Eli the priest saw Hannah's lips move but heard nothing. He mistook her anguish for drunkenness and started to scold her, adding more emotional abuse.

Hannah replied, "No, my lord, I am a woman despairing in spirit; I have drunk neither wine nor strong drink, but I have poured out my soul before the Lord." Her tears across her face as she spoke confirmed her words.

Eli softened. He told her to go in peace and added his desire that God answer her prayers.

> **Today's Peace Step**
> Pray for inner peace and be willing to let go of what you want.

Once Hannah left, she ate and no longer looked sad. She had peace from sharing her burden with God. The words of Eli probably added to her hope that God would answer this time. That peace would stay with her, and her trust in God replaced the sadness. She gave birth to a son the following year.

No More Troubles

Blessed is everyone who fears the LORD, who walks in His ways. PSALM 128:1

Jeffrey cried, "I have no more Troubles."

His mom hugged him while other people laughed. A family friend said, "We all wish we could say that! I'm sorry you've lost your little stuffed dog."

Jeff's mom said, "You must have dropped him at your cousin's house when you played. They will probably find Troubles tomorrow. You can choose one of my animals for tonight."

Jeff said, "You don't have any."

"They are in a special treasure box. I've saved them because each one reminds me of someone who blessed me with it as a gift." Jeff followed his mom to her closet, where she opened a special box filled with stuffed animals. He chose a polar bear wearing a blue vest.

Jeff's mom said, "I know you miss Troubles, but when I'm sad I think of all my blessings. God gave me so many blessings. He gave me you and your brother for sons, and Daddy for my husband. I'm blessed that we have a nice little house and food to eat."

Jeff said, "I'm blessed that my cousin will babysit tonight. She's fun."

Mom said, "Tonight your cousin will play with you for a while, and then she'll tuck you in bed and pray with you. I need to leave with Daddy and our friends.

They hugged. Jeff clutched the bear, ran to his cousin, and said, "I've got a new game we can play."

> **Today's Peace Step:**
> When you don't have inner peace, count your blessings.

They enjoyed the game with lots of laughter until bedtime.

The next day Jeff's cousin found Troubles and returned him to Jeff, who jumped up and down with joy and hugged his fluffy stuffed dog.

George Mueller (Historic Story)

The grace of the Lord Jesus Christ, and the love of God, and the fellowship of the Holy Spirit be with you all.
2 CORINTHIANS 13:14

George chose a life of sin although he had trained to be a preacher. He spent time in prison and tried to reform but failed. A friend shared about a prayer meeting, and George felt like this might be the treasure he'd been seeking all his life. He didn't understand the joy he saw and apologized for coming. The group invited him to remain and said, "Our house and hearts are open to you." He stayed and felt happy. He realized that nothing in life compared to that evening.

George continued to pray, read the Bible, and study. He wanted to be a missionary, but his father would not support him. He prayed from the heart and felt a great peace from God. An opportunity came for him to teach German to American professors who provided the needed income to finish seminary. He moved to England and began preaching. He married and chose to not request a salary. George and his wife only told God about their needs. God always provided.

Today's Peace Step:
Pray for the needs of others and trust God to respond.

George and his wife heard the account of a poor orphan boy taken to a poorhouse, which led them to start day schools for the poor and then an orphanage. He trusted God for the money, land, and houses, so the orphanages would be a testimony to God's ability to provide. On nights when they had no food for the next morning, they prayed and trusted.

One time, George had 300 children sit in the dining hall, with no food in sight. Within minutes a baker delivered three batches of bread he believed God wanted him to donate. A milkman's cart broke down in front of the orphanage, so he gifted them the milk since it would spoil otherwise. George established five homes that cared for 10,000 orphans.

Mama Didn't Smile on That Happy Day

"Do not worry about tomorrow; for tomorrow will worry about itself. Each day has enough trouble of its own." MATTHEW 6:34

Karen's mother didn't smile on her wedding day, although Karen's husband was everything Marie had dreamed of for her daughter. The day before the wedding Karen's mentally handicapped brother lost his job of waiting on tables at a school cafeteria. Although social workers could easily place him in a new position, her mom remained focused on that problem the entire day.

One problem can seem larger than life and larger than God. That can cause someone to miss out on joy as they let the problem disrupt inner peace.

Years later, when Karen's mother suffered a stroke and two cerebral hemorrhages, Karen expected her mother would never smile again. Surprise! Her mom laughed and became a more grateful woman. As families and friends surrounded her, her infirmities didn't seem to matter. She said, "I am so thankful that Dad and all of you did not desert me but stayed by my side." She started looking up jokes on the computer and sharing those as well as happy childhood memories. She also thought of three reasons to be grateful each day.

She overcame her greatest hidden fears—the fears of loss and rejection—when loved ones remained loyal. During the Great Depression, as a child, her parents had lost so much. She overlooked how happy they remained and that they trusted God and just started over. She only remembered that Christmas meant they'd repaint her dollhouse and her brother's wooden truck. She had always worried about money and overlooked how her parents laughed in spite of financial difficulties. They overcame their money losses and started a new business that thrived. At last, Marie had an inner peace, trusted in God to keep her content, and laughed often.

> **Today's Peace Step:**
> Look beyond problems to God's faithfulness and love.

Week 3

Peace with the Past, Present, and Future

Prayer for God's Peace at All Times

Father, in days of silence may I trust that you are in control always—past, present, and future. You not only created all things, but you hold them together by your power. There is nothing beyond your control and care. You love me, and all believers, totally. Forgive me when I forget to trust you.

At the same time, Lord, you tell me that you have forgiven and forgotten my past sins. You died for my sins. Your forgiveness takes away any guilt. You said I am "not guilty."

You have also said you will be with me always. That means every minute now and in the future. I ask for your Holy Spirit to guide my thinking. May I not fix my mind and heart on life's pressures, but on your promises both now and forever.

May I not dwell on past hurts, but forgive. May I not worry about the future, but trust. May I let go of fear and know You will always be with me.

Wisdom from Young Peacemakers

Life can take many paths, and we don't know where it will lead at our age. Focus on current goals and don't worry about the future.

Your Father Knows

"But seek first His kingdom and His righteousness, and all these things will provided to you." MATTHEW 6:33

Suzy watched the children at play. It resembled a type of dance. They seemed to move to a melody she couldn't hear, a cadence not unlike a waltz.

A couple of maidens wore pink ballerina outfits. Others were decked in shades of yellow, gold, purple, and rose, every gown suitable for Cinderella's ball. Surely, Suzy thought, these young ladies belong to the same family. Their garments speak of a single designer, someone who gave meticulous care to their creation.

Suddenly, she felt the caress of a breeze. The damsels twirled and curtsied. A grand ending. And, for Suzy, it was a finale because she realized the dance of the pansies in her flower bed had just offered her a type of melody for her heart.

It's so easy to be caught up in the pressures of life. We worry about the future and relive the failures and disappointments of the past. Sometimes the two collide and bring us to a type of anxiety or depression we hate to even admit to.

Thankfully, our heavenly Father is not only aware, but offers an answer. He says not to worry about our life. In Matthew 6:25–34, Jesus gave examples of our worry patterns regarding what we shall eat, drink, or wear and, of course, other passages speak to additional worries that seem to consume us.

Jesus then pointed the believer to the birds and the lilies. Birds don't sow, reap, or store food, but our heavenly

Father feeds them. Lilies don't labor or spin, yet God dresses them far better than King Solomon.

When anxiety tried to overwhelm Suzy that day, God simply drew her outside to pansies in the flower bed. Watching His creation at play reminded her of those relevant words. Yes, our heavenly Father knows and beckons us to seek His kingdom first and trust He will give us what we need. Then we'll have inner peace.

> **Today's Peace Step**
> Take a time-out to enjoy God's creation. Allow the Lord to speak to you through His world and His Word.

Is Forgiveness Possible? (Biblical Story)

If we confess our sins, He is faithful and righteous, so that He will forgive us our sins and cleanse us from all unrighteousness. 1 JOHN 1:9

Question: Do you every feel as though you've wandered too far from the Lord to be restored? Has some particular sin caused you to doubt His love and forgiveness? If so, it's time to remember what Jesus taught His disciples after His resurrection. Disciples gathered in a locked room out of fear when Jesus suddenly appeared before them with these words: "Peace be with you!"

Think about it. Before Jesus died Peter denied he knew Him three times. When he realized what he did, Peter wept but did not see Jesus to ask forgiveness before Jesus died. After their disappearance from the cross and Peter's denial, Jesus not only offered them peace and forgiveness. He went even further and sent them out as missionaries to the world.

Jesus did more for His friends. One disciple missed the meeting. When the other disciples shared the good news with Thomas, he reacted in unbelief and even said, "Unless I see the nail marks in His hands and put my finger where the nails were and put my hand into His side, I will not believe it."

One week later the room was locked again, and this time Thomas was present. Jesus appeared without using the door. He met every demand from doubting Thomas. Jesus said, "Put your finger here; see My hands. Reach out your hand and put it into My side. Stop doubting and believe."

Today's Peace Step

If a particular sin is tormenting you today, believe God forgives you and accept His peace.

How did Thomas react? He replied, "My Lord and my God!"

So, whenever we doubt God's love and forgiveness may we trust that God listens and wants us to trust. May we, like Thomas, say, "My Lord and my God!"

Not 'Member

I, I alone, am the one who wipes out your wrongdoings for My own sake, And I will not remember your sins. ISAIAH 43:25

When Sara's firstborn daughter was about five or six years old, they would sometimes ask her if she remembered a particular event from her toddlerhood. She would usually look up and say, "Not 'member." Of course, the event had happened, but she did not recall it. Sometimes her parents would retrieve an album from a nearby cabinet and turn to a picture of the event. Often, then, she would nod with a smile of recollection and want to see more of the collection. She loved seeing herself smiling and happily beside her parents or her sister.

What if we were to save pictures and other items from our children's past mistakes and failures? Certainly, this would not be a sign of good parenting. It could make our children feel sad and ashamed. No, Christian parents want to reflect a heart like our Savior. We want to celebrate the joys and forget the mistakes that we forgave.

God forgives and then promises He will not remember them. He will not bring our forgiven sins back up to us. Our minds want to replay them at times and cause us to feel guilt all over again. If that happens, we need to say, "I will not replay this forgiven sin." He wants us to smile at the future and know we can follow Him better each day.

God wants us to move forward with a new start. He wants us to have peace of mind with our past forgiven. He wants us to recall that He loved us then and loves us now and will love us always.

> **Today's Peace Step**
> When past sins pop up, say, "God does not remember," because I am forgiven.

Forgiveness frees us from the past! We're free to begin again without guilt and make better choices. Choose joy today, and choose how to live in a way that makes God smile and brings peace of mind.

A Shipwreck (Historic Story)

After you have suffered for a little while, the God of all grace, who called you to His eternal glory in Christ, will Himself perfect, confirm, strengthen, and establish you. 1 PETER 5:10

As he traveled by ship from Africa to Liverpool, the slave trader John Newton was suddenly caught up in a violent storm off the coast of Donegal, Ireland. Although Newton had been an atheist all of his life, he now cried out for God's mercy and lived! God spared him.

Newton reached Lough Swilly in Ireland safely and continued in the slave trade for six years. Having treated the slaves despicably for a long time, Newton began reading his Bible and gradually began to offer them more sympathy and understanding. In 1787 Newton wrote a tract supporting the abolition of slavery, and over time he not only became a Christian, but an Anglican priest in the Church of England.

> **Today's Peace Step**
> When you think you have failed, ask God for grace and forgiveness.

Over the years Newton wrote many hymns, but the one most loved is "Amazing Grace." This hymn represents John Newton's own spiritual journey, and the lyrics help point others out of darkness into God's light and salvation. Grace means the undeserved love and favor of

God. Read the words to his famous song here and consider how God has worked in your life and how His grace has changed you.

Has God used some dramatic event to change your life? If not, maybe you can see how He has worked overtime to help you grow spiritually. Thank God for His amazing grace.

Words of Amazing Grace

Amazing grace! how sweet the sound
That saved a wretch like me!
I once was lost, but now am found.
Was blind, but now I see.

'Twas grace that taught my heart to fear,
And grace my fears relieved;
How precious did that grace appear
The hour I first believed!

Through many dangers, toils, and snares,
I have already come;
'Tis grace hath brought me safe thus far,
And grace will lead me home.

When we've been there ten thousand years,
Bright shining as the sun,
We've no less days to sing God's praise
Than when we first begun.

Destined for Failure or Recovery?

Rejoice always, pray continually, give thanks in all cir-cumstances; for this is God's will for you in Christ Jesus.
1 THESSALONIANS 5:16–18 (NIV)

John ran into trouble in his mid-teens in a small town in New Jersey. One afternoon John waited in the car while some friends picked up some items from a convenience store. "Picked up" turned out to be an appropriate phrase since John's friends had not paid for the items. As it turned out someone caught the number on the car tag and police apprehended the boys for shoplifting.

Sometime later the authorities became convinced of John's innocence. He had been permitted to live with relatives in Alabama under the authority of the Alabama Department of Youth Services on the Thomasville, Alabama, campus. The counselors at the behavior modification facility worked at helping him make good choices.

> **Today's Peace Step**
>
> Remember someone who helped mold your character and sent you in a godly direction. Thank them and the Lord.

One day, when John had almost completed his assignment there, his counselor commented. "John," he said. "You are a good physical specimen. Do you play football?"

"No, sir," John answered.

"Then here's my suggestion. When you go back to school next week give it a try."

John followed up on the idea, made the cut, and played for the last two years of high school. He had a knack for catching, throwing, and running fast. He enjoyed the sport and his teammates. He became a good player. In fact, he even earned a scholarship to Auburn and a slot on the Southeast Conference Academic Team. More than once, John sent pictures and thank-you notes to his former counselors. He showed gratitude to people God used to help mold his character. Once considered a juvenile delinquent, John Davis became a successful businessman. John made peace with his past, present, and future.

Week 4

Havens of Peace

A Prayer for Calm in His Care

Father, as your child, I realize you are the source of life and peace. Nothing escapes your notice and concern. I often act as if I am in control and then realize I am not. Forgive me for forgetting that you are God.

In your Word you have compared me, and all of us, to lost and helpless sheep. However, you also call yourself our Good Shepherd. Like a lost lamb, I often make a choice that causes problems, say words that hurt someone, or waste my time on myself. I ask you to care for me like a good shepherd takes care of the little lambs. May your presence give me peace today.

I trade peace for worry and let my wants and my concerns crowd out the beauty and blessings around me. Help me be calm and know that problems come and go but that you stay with me. Guide me today and every day until I see you face to face in the perfect haven of peace.

Wisdom from Young Peacemakers

A bit of time alone is good.

I go to my room and play with my hamster.

Bomb Threat

The LORD is for me; I will not fear; What can man do to me?
PSALM 118:6

A bomb? What kind of maniac would plant a bomb in a Christian school? As Aria drove the children home she couldn't believe what they told her.

"Mama," her first grader exclaimed, "they said to leave immediately."

"Let me tell some of it," her fourth grader interrupted. "They sent for the police and fire department. Everybody stood outside while they searched every inch of the building. When everybody decided it was safe they let us go back in."

"How long were you outside?"

"About an hour."

As the carpool children continued to chatter Aria drove home in meditative silence. She remembered all the times she had prayed for the children going to and from school. It had never occurred to pray for their safety during school hours.

It was sometime that night before she heard the full story of the bomb threat. Several schools in their city had had a similar scare. It seems the children of a prominent political figure were the target for harassment. The bomb squad discovered one bomb in a nearby school, but it had been deactivated and everyone remained unharmed. Later that evening Aria's friend Ellen phoned and they exchanged reactions to the day's events.

"What did Elizabeth say about the bomb?" Aria inquired. "Was she upset?"

"Not too much. In fact, her maturity surprised everyone. She said, 'Mother, I wanted to take my Bible outside with me during the alarm. Then I remembered I could take God. I said, no matter what happens, even if the whole school blows up, God will be with me. No, I wasn't too afraid.'"

Aria's mind fixed on Elizabeth's statement. All afternoon she had bemoaned the perplexities and fears of the modern world. Elizabeth showed greater wisdom. She had zeroed in on God. Bomb threat. You name it. God is greater and with us. Can we ask for anything more?

A Shepherd for the Soul (Biblical Story)

My sheep listen to My voice, and I know them, and they follow Me. JOHN 10:27

Sara enjoys wearing a certain ring. For one thing, the amethyst stone matches many of her outfits. More importantly, it belonged to her precious grandmother. Sara recalls during childhood, sitting beside her, staring at old, crooked fingers but then concentrating on the tenderness and love in those hands. Soon her eyes settled on the ring, never dreaming it would one day be hers. Now her fingers have curled and become crooked to match!

The passage today talks about something greater than a ring or old hands. It speaks of a shepherd who tenderly cares for his beloved sheep. Yes, Sara's grandmother gave her a ring, but God gives her peace. Grandmother was snatched from her loved ones years ago, but as a believer, she was never snatched from God's hands. In Christ, the same is true for all believers.

Sara loves that Christ refers to us as sheep. Sheep are helpless, stubborn, and unpredictable critters, and so are we. We are easily confused and prone to wander. How often, Lord, do we feel like sheep? We tend to wander.

Sometimes earthly shepherds are neglectful. Not Christ. They may not recognize or take advantage of the best pasture. Not Christ.

Today's Peace Step

Remember the Lord is your Shepherd. No one can snatch you from His hands.

He leads us to fruitful places. If a sheep is lost, some shepherds might say, "So be it," and move on. Not Christ. He is always watching us and ready to answer when we need help.

When peace seems to slip away, read Psalm 23 that shares how God is our shepherd. Note all the things He does for you with His hands. Pray that you will be a lamb who follows and be thankful you have a handy Shepherd.

Lesson in a Storm

For you have not received a spirit of slavery leading to fear again, but you have received a spirit of adoption as sons and daughters by which we cry out, "Abba! Father!" ROMANS 8:15

Many years ago, a pastor shared one of his most memorable experiences. While on a long flight a warning light flashed: "Fasten your seat belts." Soon a calm voice said, "We shall not be serving beverages since we are expecting a little turbulence. Please be sure your seat belt is fastened."

Later the voice returned with, "We are sorry, but we won't be serving the meal at this time. The turbulence is still ahead."

As the minister looked around, he noticed the apprehensive faces of many passengers. In fact, he began to feel it a bit himself. Minutes later the storm broke. Lightning. Thunder. Soon the plane felt like a cork being tossed on a celestial ocean, lifted by currents of air one moment and then tossed downward as if about to crash.

The pastor said, "I looked around again and could see that nearly all the passengers were alarmed. Some appeared to be praying. Would they make it through the storm?"

"Then," he said, "my eyes fell on a little girl. Apparently the storm held no fear for her. She had tucked her feet beneath her and was calmly reading a book. Sometimes she closed her eyes. Then she would

> **Today's Peace Step**
> When storms come, and they will, we need not be a slave again to fear if we trust in our heavenly Father.

stretch her legs and read again. No worry seemed to invade her world. As the plane rose and fell and the adults seemed scared to death, this marvelous child remained composed and unafraid. I could hardly believe my eyes."

When the plane finally reached its destination and the relieved passengers hurried off, the pastor lingered behind to see the little girl. After commenting about the storm and the erratic plane, he asked, "Why weren't you afraid?"

"Oh," the child replied, "I wasn't afraid 'cause my Daddy is the pilot, and he's taking me home."

Faith that Brings Peace (Historic Story)

But God, being rich in mercy, because of His great love with which He loved us, even when we were dead in our wrongdoings, made us alive together with Christ (by grace you have been saved). EPHESIANS 2:4–5

Dr. Martyn Lloyd-Jones, a former pastor of Westminster Chapel in London and the author of several books, told a story about himself as a young Christian.

Eager to learn, Jones met with some older and wiser friends to discuss faith and theology. One day the topic focused on, "What is the essence of being a believer in Christ?"

Someone turned to Martyn and asked, "What do you think, Jones? How would you define what happens in a believer's heart?"

Surprised, Jones stammered, "Well, I . . ." Then inhaling deeply, he continued: "That's hard. In fact, I suppose it would take the rest of the day to explain it."

An older woman in the group gently chided him with, "Oh, no, Martyn. You are an heir of salvation. Purchased by God. Born of His Holy Spirit. Washed in His blood."

These words sound strange now but speak of God saving us so we will live in heaven.

Silence filled the room as all pondered the accuracy and beauty of this lady's reply. It's true. Believers don't have to be astute in theology to define the faith. One way may be to just joyfully sing "Blessed Assurance." The word assurance means you can count on it. Yes, you can have peace always once you believe and trust in God.

> **Today's Peace Step**
> Be prepared to explain your faith simply and why that brings inner peace.

For the rest of his life, Martyn Lloyd-Jones expounded the faith in depth, beauty, and simplicity. God blessed his congregation for many years, and his work still teaches and inspires today. We can rejoice with both old and new songs about God's power, love, and peace.

Wipe-Out Worry

Having cast all your anxiety on Him, because He cares about you. 1 PETER 5:7

Three-year-old Cherie tossed in her bed, so her mother went to check. Her forehead felt warm. What now? It was late January, and her family of four had been in and out of sick bay for six weeks.

"Honey," her mother whispered. "Come let Mama hold you."

"Aw right," she said, climbing into the rocker.

"Cherie, I'm sorry you aren't feeling well." Her voice was heavy with anxiety.

"That's aw right, mamma. We pray 'bout it, then you won't haf to worry."

Isn't that the root of much of our trouble? Worry? "We pray . . . ," she said.

Prayer takes time, and time is precious. Our schedules seem full. The clock is ticking. The guests will arrive soon. We worry and forget to toss that aside and be thankful people will come.

Children are full of details and come running to share. In love, we listen, share, and interact. How much more God cares about us. But, too often, we forget to pray.

When we get to the end of ourselves, He wants us to come. But we are helpless every day. In God's sight we're like the infant crying in the crib.

No, I'm a responsible adult. I can reason and manipulate. A war goes on within us, and it won't cease until we fall on our knees and confess. Until we remember to give God the anxiety.

Today's Peace Step
Ask God to replace your fear with peace.

When we each admit "I'm helpless," we remember to trust God for every need. We can tell Him everything. He will calm our hearts. We can thank God for the food we have to serve (another lesson from a child). Let us remember the words of a three-year-old theologian, "We pray 'bout it, then you won't haf to worry.'"

Week 5

Emotional Peace

Prayer to Calm Our Emotions

Dear Lord, my emotions go up and down and change as fast as a roller coaster some days. When things go wrong or anyone argues, it can topple my day. Help me to trust in you and not little things in life. You are unchanging, and your love is always free and limitless.

You call me to be strong and courageous because you will be with me. Still, bad news can send me reeling or cause fear to rise inside of me. Help me know that nothing surprises you and that you are already prepared to guide me through whatever happens.

I thank you for pleasant days and loved ones who bring joy into my life and lift my spirits. Thank you for your constant presence that assures me I can have peace within, a peace that others do not understand. You are my source of calm in life's storms. Knowing you have brought me through many problems gives me confidence that you will bring me through any challenges I will face this week.

Wisdom from Young Peacemakers

On a good day I don't scream or kick anyone.

When I'm sad, my brother makes me laugh and then my whole face smiles.

Angry Heart

Do not let sin control the way you live; do not give in to sinful desires. ROMANS 6:12 (NLT)

Daniel stomped in with his fists clenched and yelled, "I can't stop my anger."

Mom hugged him and said, "Let's pray. Lord, help Daniel be calm. Give him a verse or idea that will always help him go from anger to peace in his heart."

Daniel took a few slow breaths and counted his fingers. He stomped outside and ran around the yard. He exercised with jumping jacks, climbed his favorite trees, and swung on a swing. He came in and said, "Mom, please read some jokes." She read a few from a book, and they both started laughing.

Daniel said, "I feel better, but I hate being teased. Sometimes nothing you and Dad told me to do helps me calm down." He went to his room to play.

Later Daniel raced into the kitchen and yelled, "Mommy, Jesus gave me a verse. It's Romans 6:12. I know that will help me not be angry again." He skipped off to play.

> **Today's Peace Step**
> Ask God to give you a verse that helps you have inner peace.

Daniel's mom thought, *Lord, I would never have chosen that verse, but you know my son even better than I do. We have tried so many techniques to help him be calm and feel peace in his heart. I'll pray that verse works and that he'll always remember it.*

The next day Daniel walked in with a big grin. He said, "Today when I played with the kids outside, I stayed calm. Even when one of them teased me, I remembered the verse Jesus gave me and just laughed. Satan won't control me anymore."

Mom said, "That's good. I'm thankful God knows what Scripture will help you the most." She noticed Daniel always remained peaceful after that day.

Emotional Martha (Biblical Story, based on John 11:1–12:8)

But the Lord answered and said to her, "Martha, Martha, you are worried and distracted by many things." LUKE 10:41

Martha argued over the possible stench of her brother's tomb, complained that her sister did not help with meal preparations, and spoke from grief that her brother had died. She had welcomed Jesus and sent word when her brother became ill. She placed her hope in Jesus to heal her brother but also let her emotions show freely through her words.

Feelings are natural. However, we can control how we respond and what we say as we face both joys and struggles. Jesus, as stated in John 11:5, loved Martha and her siblings. He responded with patience and love. He quietly corrected her to change her perspective in viewing her sister as someone who supported Him and showed her joy at His presence. He wanted Martha to make great choices and be at peace with herself and her family.

After telling the disciples that Lazarus was sleeping and letting Martha know her brother would rise, Jesus heard Mary state that her brother would not have died if Jesus had been there. Facing the disbelief of His closest friends and their grief at the loss they perceived, Jesus wept. Grief and words that revealed a lack of faith moved Him as He stood at the tomb. Then Jesus did what He always knew He would do: He brought Lazarus back to life. Everyone's sorrow turned to joy.

> **Today's Peace Step**
>
> Use your talents in what you enjoy and rejoice with others who choose to do what they enjoy.

A few days later Martha did what she enjoyed; she served Jesus and the others. Mary did what she enjoyed; she washed the feet of Jesus with expensive perfume. Lazarus reclined at the table with Jesus. That depicts a harmonious family.

Jesus sat in the midst of the family, a grateful family, who lived in peace.

Tongue Tied

And my God will supply all your needs according to His riches in glory in Christ Jesus. PHILIPPIANS 4:19

The phone rang. "Hello, Mrs. W. This is the school nurse. Your daughter, Rebecca, fell. They rushed her to the base clinic. Please meet her there."

Karen hung up the phone and called her husband. She phoned a neighbor to watch her younger children. She raced out and across the golf course, praying, as tears rolled down her cheeks. Blood covered her daughter's face and clothes. Her husband rushed in as a doctor said, "They call me Mad Dog Jack. Your daughter bit through her tongue. She needs stitches."

Their dentist, also in the room, said, "Only an oral surgeon can do that." They could only get off their tiny island by ferry boat or helicopter. The clinic had no oral surgeon.

Jack grinned. "You're in luck. We're holding our annual oral surgeon conference here. I'll stitch her tongue, and these other surgeons will watch. It's good training for war zones."

Rebecca's mom replied, "It's not luck. We prayed before Rebecca left home for God to supply all her needs today." She thought, *My heart is calm again.*

Back home she thanked her neighbor and said Becky's mouth will be swollen for a few days, so she can only drink shakes, very soft food, and frozen sorbet. Her oldest son said, "Mom, Becky looks like the Incredible Hulk. How'd you do that?" She laughed, then recalled her in-laws were coming to visit.

> **Today's Peace Step**
> Start your day
> with prayer and
> thanksgiving.

She panicked at the mess the little ones had made and thought of the food she had not cooked and panicked again. A friend brought over homemade nondairy shakes for Rebecca, remembering her dairy allergies. She also helped clean up. Company arrived and pitched in. Rebecca's friends often asked her to stick out her tongue to fact-check that no scar formed since the tongue is always moist. They continued to pray and thank God every morning for supplying their needs.

Turned Off and then Turned on Again (Historic Story)

And whatever you ask in My name, this I will do, so that the Father may be glorified in the Son. JOHN 14:13

"I began at last to think that for some reason or other I could not be saved, and that the best I could do was to take my fill of this world, as there was no hope for me beyond the grave." The great missionary to the Chinese people, Hudson Taylor, held this belief in his teen years. His parents prayed for him and with him from birth. They lived their faith, but as often as Hudson tried to become a Christian, he failed.

He engaged with skeptics who questioned people who professed faith in the Bible and lived as though it didn't exist. He felt that if he could believe the Bible, he would certainly try to live it. Unknown to him, his sister committed to pray for his faith. Soon after she started her daily prayer, Hudson, alone and bored one afternoon, picked up a tract and thought, *There will be a story at the commencement, and a sermon or moral at the close: I will take the former and leave the latter for those who like it.* He considered the serious looks of believers too stern and the words too prosy.

He read, and in reflecting, understood the words, "It is finished," meant that Jesus paid our debts for sin. He wondered if all was finished, what could he add or do? Joy flooded his soul, and he knelt and started to praise Jesus. He believed and accepted Jesus. However, over time Hudson's joy gave way to conflict until he asked God to give him work to do, a purpose. He felt God's presence and a lasting great joy. Within a month he felt impressed that God wanted him to be a missionary in China. He

> **Today's Peace Step**
> Ask for God's guidance and follow it.

studied Scriptures and lived on one-third of his income to prepare himself.

Hudson Taylor spent fifty-one years in China, where he followed God's call. He started 125 schools and brought 800 missionaries there.

Washed Away

Have I not commanded you? Be strong and courageous! Do not be terrified nor dismayed, for the LORD your God is with you wherever you go. JOSHUA 1:9

"I can't do it. I've never driven our new van. You and my dad could die. It's manual steering and has a standard transmission." Karen sobbed.

Flooding rain and wind washed away the gravel and dirt from half the driveway, leaving a huge ditch. Jim needed to return to work to fly out for a meeting. The paved upper driveway had remained firm, keeping the cars safe. They had spent the entire day filling in the newly formed ravine by hauling railroad ties and old tires from the nearby woods. The children laughed as they rolled the tires and then filled buckets with rocks and dirt, and dumped them in. Being five months pregnant, Karen carried light loads of fill. Her mother brought out snacks and drinks. They filled about half the space all the way down the drive.

Jim jumped up and down on the fill to press it in. The children jumped too. He felt they had just enough room to drive it out but thought it better for his father-in-law and him to push on the side of the van and let Karen drive. They needed to finish before dark. With a stream on one side and the unfilled ditch on the other she needed to squeeze along the filled area.

> **Today's Peace Step**
> Overcome your fears with trusting God.

Jim prayed with Karen and said, "Practice on the paved area until you feel you can drive the van, then start driving down the path. It's wide enough. She prayed as she drove and kept repeating, "I trust you, Lord." She wanted to close her eyes but knew she had to focus and not hit the brakes to avoid sliding. She reached the road's paved shoulder, stopped, turned off the engine, and jumped out of the van. She hugged both men. Everyone rejoiced.

Week 6

Peace in Grief and Loss

Prayer during Times of Loss

Lord, I never imagined how tragedy could change my life. I know sorrow comes to every home at some point. Yet, when it is my grief, it seems so hard, and I feel so shattered. Then I wonder how others overcome the pain within.

Loss of a loved one, pet, job, health, and more are real and difficult. Your words remind us that you heal the broken and wounded, but sometimes it takes a long time to heal and leaves scars on our hearts. The pain lessens, but we forever miss the person or thing we lost.

Even in our careers, we gain a new job, but when there's a job lost it cuts into our ego and takes a while to realize you wanted to redirect us. Help us to turn to you in our grief and let you show us how to cope, overcome, and smile again.

Let me be mindful of the loss other people sustain and be willing to pray and listen. No two people grieve the same way. Let us not offer platitudes but simply help where needed.

Even now you know my future sorrows, and I trust them to you. Help me when the time comes to trust and wait on your timing.

Wisdom from Young Peacemakers

I feel better when I sing.

I need a kiss to feel better.

Peace for a Heart Shattered by Grief

The LORD is near to the brokenhearted and saves those who are crushed in spirit. PSALM 34:18

Blond hair with bangs that swept across his crystal blue eyes remain a strong memory of her son. Once Rhonda Robinson thought that if God had said before her son Danny was born, "I'm going to give you this intelligent creative, young man, and he will be a delight to your heart for thirteen years, and that's all you get with him, and you will mourn him the rest of your life," she realized she would do it all over again.

That conclusion helped her be grateful for what she had and heal from her overwhelming grief. The unimaginable loss of her son left her heart shattered. Her healing came with trusting God and not through asking questions.

Rhonda told Danny to stay home and turned down his request to go with her to be at her daughter's side for surgery. But her older son invited him to play basketball with their friends, and that turned to tragedy on the road. It ended Danny creating wonderful stories.

> **Today's Peace Step**
> Invite God's peace into your pain.

Ambulances at the accident scene took the boys to four different hospitals. Only Danny died. She felt like a trust between God and her had been broken along with her heart and that God robbed her of her son.

Rhonda also felt like she faced the spiritual equivalent to Newton's law where there's an equal and opposite reaction to every action. The force of God's peace equaled the amount of her pain. She heard God's voice louder than at any other time of her life. We live in a fallen world where the unspeakable happens. She recalls when Danny asked how to go to heaven, and she explained it to him. He accepted Christ and believed.

Rhonda discovered that when she focused on her loss, she lost what she had, and it was like sinking sand sorrow. When she focused on what she had with gratitude, she gained what she'd lost. It's a process that brought peace and led to her book *Freefall*.

Jesus and Loss

Jesus wept. JOHN 11:35

Before the death of John the Baptist, Jesus told His disciples that John had been raised from the dead, so miracle powers worked in him (Mark 6:14). He referred to baptism. When John's disciples complained about Jesus's preaching, John said, "He must increase, but I must decrease." He knew God numbered his days. When Herod had John beheaded, Jesus withdrew to be alone.

When Lazarus became ill, Jesus knew he'd raise Lazarus from dead. In John 11:4 Jesus said, "Lazarus's sickness will not end in death. No, it happened for the glory of God so that the Son of God will receive glory from this."

When Jairus, an official from the synagogue, came and asked Jesus to heal his daughter, Jesus started to walk to the home of the girl. As He approached someone came from the home of Jairus and declared that the girl had died. Jesus told Jairus in Luke 8:49–56 to "believe and she will be made well." He proclaimed to mourners, "She had not died, but is asleep." He healed her.

These accounts of Jesus and deaths reveal the heart of Jesus that welled up from love, loss, and more. He tried so hard to have His closest friends and others really listen and believe in Him. Before raising Lazarus, Jesus stated, "I am the resurrection." His eyes teared up quietly in contrast to the loud wailing of mourners. He kept everyone out when He raised the young girl. He always knows the final outcome and understands our grief when we lose a loved one who is not healed.

> **Today's Peace Step**
> Believe in God's unlimited power to help us have peace.

How often do we limit God in our thoughts or struggle about a death? We know what He did on earth and know what He's done for us in the past. We know that the ultimate deed we can do is to bring God glory; sometimes that happens in healing and sometimes in death. Jesus wants us to trust the outcomes to Him and have faith that God is really almighty.

Loss of Dreams

"For I know the plans that I have for you," declares the LORD, "plans for prosperity and not for disaster, to give you a future and a hope. JEREMIAH 29:11

Not one offer of residency. After the years of schooling and all the applications, Joe didn't receive any offers. Elizabeth also felt heartbroken seeing her husband watch his dreams fall apart. They tried for a few years while Joe took whatever jobs he could find.

With a growing family, life seemed to deal one tough punch after another. Each attempt at a new career path dissolved, and Elizabeth had a hard time watching her husband get crushed again and again. The hardest part came when they had to ask their parents for help and continued to need help to pay bills. Overwhelmed with debt, they looked into bankruptcy, but even that meant needing a few thousand dollars and experiencing lots of stigmas and restrictions.

They always clung to God and continued to tithe. Finally, Joe found a one-year accelerated nursing program and humbly applied. They knew they had no way to buy a house in the foreseeable future and already owned a car and other big items needed, so they took the plunge into bankruptcy, because that would help them move beyond the money problems. They had avoided that for years, because it would have affected someone who had cosigned a student loan with them, but that person passed away. They believed God was showing them a

> **Today's peace step**
> Persist even when dreams shatter; look for a new path.

new path. Bankruptcy brought a deep peace as it relieved them of money problems while revealing a brighter future with a different career.

Elizabeth found a job as a shopper where she earned enough to pay the bills and still homeschool their five children. As Joe finished the nursing program the pandemic hit, and no one was hiring nurses in his area. God blessed Elizabeth's income by doubling it. They saved to move. They rejoice daily since they moved a few states away where he did get a job offer, and Joe loves nursing.

Russell Conwell and Johnny Ring (Historic Story)

And do not be conformed to this world, but be transformed by the renewing of your mind, so that you may prove what the will of God is, that which is good and acceptable and perfect. ROMANS 12:2

Captain Russell Conwell demanded that his orderly, Johnny Ring, stop reading the Bible, saying, "It is full of lies."

"My mother made me promise I would," the teen replied. He served the captain and cared for his sword. Another time the captain said, "Do not pray in my tent." Johnny continued to read the Bible and pray, but he did so outside the tent.

Whiz! Bullets flew. *Boom!* Cannon balls exploded as rebels attacked Union soldiers while the captain was away. Johnny raced across a bridge into the tent engulfed in flames and grabbed the sword. No one stopped him as he ran through the flames back across the bridge. Flames burned his flesh, but he hugged the sword, collapsed into a friend's arms, and said, "Give the captain his sword." He died three days later.

A month later enemy fire hit Captain Conwell. The captain survived and asked the chaplain to read some of the passages that Johnny had read. He later wrote how an instinctive need for God filled him, he asked God to reveal Himself, and then forgiveness filled his soul with light. He dedicated his life to God.

Every morning Conwell prayed, "Lord, if thou wilt help me today, I will do Johnny Ring's work and my work." Conwell built Temple University and directed two hospitals. He worked

> **Today's Peace Step**
> Be respectful
> of other people
> and their faith.

sixteen-hour days—eight hours for himself and eight in honor of Johnny, the young man he never forgot. The rescued sword remains mounted on the wall of Baptist Temple at Temple University in Philadelphia where Conwell preached. On the grounds of Temple University is a green area called the Johnny Ring Garden with a statue of faithful Johnny.

Insight to Peace after Vision Loss

Your word is a lamp to my feet and a light to my path. PSALM *119:105*

The ophthalmologist said, "You have retinitis pigmentosa." At thirteen, Janet Perez Eckles learned that her inherited condition meant loss of eyesight but probably not until she reached her sixties. At age twenty-seven, with a young son and pregnant with another son, she noticed loss of night and peripheral vision. She remained in denial as she continued to drive and sought any help to improve her sight.

She tore up her eye doctor's warning to stop driving. She thought, *This happens to other people but not me.* At age thirty she lost all vision.

Looking back Janet says, "I was very prissy and caught up in my image, clothes, beautiful curls, and good looks. The thought of being a woman with a white cane horrified me." She rejected help for the blind because with three little boys she had no time for training. She figured out how to cook and keep house in her permanent state of darkness. She also found a new career, as a bilingual woman, interpreting for the courts, finding her way in the courthouse with her white cane. She rejoiced when they switched to having her work from home by phone.

Her husband, overwhelmed, left, and the stress increased. Janet sought God as a last resort. She joined a Bible study, listened to an audio Bible, and decided, "I cannot see, but I'll do what God calls me to do." Once she gave up self-pity, she found peace, and her husband returned. She made sure her boys listened to the Bible and joined children's ministry programs.

> **Today's Peace Step**
> Trust God to bring peace, no matter what happens.

Janet became an international speaker and author, sharing how with God we can be courageous, find peace, and respond to God's call. Decades later her husband took their money and left. God supplied all her needs. A few years later, Janet married a wonderful man.

Week 7

Peace through Letting Go of Control

Prayer to Let God Be in Control

Dear Lord, I like to know what's happening and take control. I want to know I can influence the outcome, although I know you are the one who knows best. I'm afraid to let go and trust you. I am restless when I need to lean on others or you, and yet time and again when I do let go, things turn out better. I am more relaxed once I let go.

Help me trust and realize that everything doesn't have to be perfect. Help me look back and realize you always choose the best for me. Even in struggles you use those times to teach me and redirect my path.

Let me rejoice as my children make their choices and trust you are with them. Help me submit my will to your perfect plans.

Wisdom from Young Peacemakers

Sometimes it's best to just walk away.

I put Mom's kiss in my heart. If I'm upset I take it out.

Letting Go by Joan Patterson

There is an appointed time for everything. And there is a time for every event under heaven. ECCLESIASTES 3:1

For ten years Joan's four-legged furry friend and she worked as a synchronized team. At the beginning, Faith sat when Joan wanted her to stand, or vice versa. Joan gave the command to come to her one side and Faith would go to the other. Practice and time transformed their partnership until Faith knew what Joan wanted before she asked.

Faith always stayed by Joan's side. Even when she had an allergic reaction, Faith rode in the ambulance with her and slept on her bed in the hospital. In public, Faith always received attention as she strode alongside Joan. People commented as the dog carried a package in her mouth. The more comments, the higher she held the package.

They were so bonded that Joan didn't notice Faith slowing down. She took longer to stand on her hind legs to turn on lights. She hesitated when loading into the car seat. She was slower getting up from her bed. Her body language told Joan she wanted to retire.

> **Today's Peace Step**
> Allow God to exchange emotional pain and hurt with His love.

How could Joan go on? She would get another dog, but it would not be Faith.

The last day Joan took off Faith's work harness Faith was so excited because it meant playtime. No longer could Faith accompany her in public places. How could Joan survive? Tears flooded her face and dripped on the harness. She grieved the end of their working relationship.

Faith remained alpha dog when Giles first came to take over her duties. As the years progressed, the roles reversed. She spent more time in bed and had more and more difficulty standing up. Her back legs didn't cooperate. One day she tried to stand and couldn't. Joan will forever remember the look on her face. It was time. She couldn't go on.

That night she calmly laid in Joan's arms as Joan watched life leave Faith's body.

Paul (Biblical Story)

[Jesus said], "Father, if You are willing, remove this cup from Me; yet not My will, but Yours be done." LUKE 22:42

Philippians is a book of joy written from Paul while in a terrible prison. Paul went from being Saul, a man riding a horse, with power and soldiers who obeyed his orders, to a missionary on foot who survived much persecution. He suffered beatings, shipwrecks, stoning, imprisonment, and more. He did it all willingly once he let go of his pride and submitted his life to God. He considered his accomplishments as nothing in comparison to knowing Jesus (3:7–8).

Paul shared from prison how he prayed with joy for the Philippians. In chapter 2 he shared how unity in faith brings joy. His perspective changed once he let go of his pride and humbly followed Jesus. In Philippians 4, Paul shared the source of his contentment and peace.

Rejoice, as Paul stated in verse 4, and let the peace of God guard your hearts. Dwell on worthy thoughts, he shared in verse 8. In prison he thought of the opportunity his situation provided for him to share the gospel with soldiers and Roman leaders.

Be content in your own circumstances, he wrote in verses 11–12. He had learned to be satisfied with what God provided, including through his friends.

> **Today's Peace Step**
> Choose to rejoice because of God's love, and trust Him to supply your needs.

Then, as stated in verse 13, trust that you can do all things through Christ. Paul could live in dire prison conditions because he had God's love. Paul lived what he preached and wrote. The letter portrays his life as joy filled. He had peace every day.

When you are feeling defeated or discouraged, read Philippians again and praise God for His presence and your blessings.

Puppet Team

For the equipping of the saints for the work of ministry, for the building up of the body of Christ. EPHESIANS 4:12

Rebecca started a puppet ministry in high school, with her mom's help. She knew she'd leave for college and prayed for ideas to make sure the ministry continued as her mom agreed to continue being a leader. She realized she could run a puppet training camp and recruit some of the team members to run different parts of it so campers could rotate through each section. That way puppeteers could take roles of leading in one area. She met with her leader recruits and found they had great ideas on how to train the campers and build the team.

The group planned a show for the campers to perform at the end of the week. They quickly realized who caught on to manipulating the puppets best and gave them lead roles, while others worked the props and easier puppet roles. It worked so well that the new leaders asked if they could continue leading performances at weekly rehearsals. Rebecca felt God led her to give up her role as director, and she worked on equipping the leaders with devotions and various aspects of leadership. A year later when she left for college, she knew the team would keep going.

> **Today's Peace Step**
> Let go of control by training your replacements.

She came home early at Christmas to watch and help the team perform at a low-income medical center. When the music stopped, the puppets froze and then restarted as the music picked back up. The kids roared. The leaders decided it might be good to leave that error in the show, and Rebecca praised them for working so well through the glitch.

Equipping those who come after us to lead produces new leaders and lets us move on to the next work God calls us to do.

Billy Graham

I have fought the good fight, I have finished the course, I have kept the faith. 2 TIMOTHY 4:7

"I would speak less and study more, and I would spend more time with my family." These words of Billy Graham remind us of the struggles we face when balancing our call from God with our family. His children grew up missing him yet knowing he loved them dearly.

Sometimes we need to let go of the perfect dreams and find peace with reality while also working to make adjustments that make a difference. Billy was away when his first child came into the world, away so long that when his eldest son was young and saw him in his mom's bed one morning he asked, "Who's he?"

Once he disciplined his daughter Gigi and then chased after her because she stomped away in anger. He scolded her harshly and she responded, "Some dad you are! You go away and leave us all the time!" Billy's eyes filled with tears as he faced the impact his choices had on her. He tried to change and be more intentional in time spent with his children. He was easier on the youngest. Ned shared how when he knocked on his dad's door he heard him say, "Just a moment, Lyndon," and then he motioned for Ned to come in.

> **Today's Peace Step**
> Be intentional with investing time in loved ones, and remain steadfast in faith.

Ned said, "To me, that said I was more important than the president of the United States!" His children wandered and struggled but all ended up serving God in ministry. He told his son Franklin during a time of rebellion that he would always love him unconditionally, that he and his mom sensed a struggle in Franklin, and that Franklin would need to make a choice. Soon after Franklin chose God.

Billy Graham remained at peace with the firm conviction that he never wavered in his commitment to serve God as an evangelist.

Letting Go without Losing Your Grip by Linda Goldfarb

Cast your burden upon the LORD and He will sustain you; He will never allow the righteous to be shaken. PSALM 55:22

The rain-drenched window matched how Julia felt inside. Refreshed. "Abba, you did it. You transformed our eggshell relationship into a fountain of love and hope."

Seven months earlier, Julia sat across from Michelle, capturing each word her twenty-six-year-old shared between intermittent sobbing. "You. Will. Hate. Me. Mom!"

Five words forever frozen in Julia's memory. *Was this a temptation to compromise her faith over her love for her daughter? No. God is sovereign.*

"Michelle, look at me," Julia placed her hand gently under Michelle's chin. "My sweet darling, no matter what, I love you. Always and forever."

"You can't love me, Mom. You talk against this all the time."

"Michelle, you know your momma's a sinner, right? I do things all the time that upset God. Yet He loves me enough to forgive me. And no matter what, I love you." Julia's eyes remained focused on her little girl.

"I'm gay, Mom."

Her eyes clouded by tears, Julia sensed Michelle's gaze. "And I love you, Michelle."

"So you're okay with it?"

Julia heard a lift in Michelle's voice. "No. I'm not okay." She prayed, *Father, give me the words, Your words.* "But I love you and always will."

The next few months gave way to continuous streams of one-sided emotional whirlwinds. Anger. Unreturned calls. Proverbial eggshells cast about daring Julia to walk on them.

One day, Julia and her husband received an Evite. "You're invited to Michelle's 30th Birthday." A riverboat day trip. Filled with Michelle's *new* friends.

Lord, I can't do this on my own. I give you my little girl. I trust you to care for her. Please help Michelle understand how much we love her. Julia's mind calmed as she tapped the "Attending" button, then pressed send.

> **Today's Peace Step**
> Let go. God has this.

As Julia and Bob returned from their daughter's birthday gathering, her phone vibrated. "No matter what, Mom, you are my first go-to. I love you for always loving me. Michelle"

Hope in a text. That's my girl. That's my God. Julia sighed.

Week 8

Peace through Gratitude

A Prayer of Constant Appreciation

Almighty God and Father, I want to live a grateful life. May other people see me smile in spite of troubles. May they see peace in place of worry.

I am amazed again today by your grace and peace. You are called the Prince of Peace, so may I constantly reflect on you and your gift of peace. Gratitude fills my heart with peace. Help me look around and see so much to appreciate in your creation and the blessings of family and home.

May I live this day in constant thankfulness. Let me reflect on the blessings I receive today and the opportunities to comfort others and help them have peace. May my heart always be filled with thanks.

Wisdom from Young Peacemakers

I made friends with Esther. I said hi and was just nice to her.

I let friends take the first turn. That makes them smile.

A Kmart Moment

Shout joyfully to the LORD, all the earth. Serve the LORD with jubilation; Come before Him with rejoicing. PSALM 100:1–2

Five-year-old Abby jumped up and down as she and her mother, Beth, entered Kmart, Abby's favorite store. After admiring some floral arrangements near the entrance, the blue light began to flash along with the announcement, "Our first special today is in the children's shoe department."

Abby clapped. "Mama! Mama, can you believe it? Let's hurry."

Abby began to pull on her mother's arm as she tried to steer their cart to the back of the store. As soon as they arrived at the first row of shoes Abby dropped to her knees and in a loud voice prayed, "Oh, thank you, Lord Jesus. You know I need shoes for school, and shoes are 'spensive. Mama said money is tight so . . . oh, how I thank you for this blue light special!"

> **Today's Peace Step**
> From the moment you wake up, focus your heart on Jesus Christ.

Abby tried on shoes and giggled if they were too big or too small. She found ones on sale in just her size. She hugged her mother.

As Beth shared her story, her girlfriend tried to imagine her facial expression following Abby's prayer. Her friend imagined Beth's face go from shock to embarrassment and then maybe erupt into a smile. At any rate, her girlfriend smiled now as Beth continued, "Sara, we've tried to teach our children to express their joy and thanksgiving every day, but I never expected this. I honestly think Abby focused more on thanking Jesus than on the prized shoes. I tend to worry about what other people think, but she wanted Jesus to have all of the glory."

Her girlfriend nodded and took Beth's hand, and they both thanked God for the lesson. Her friend said, "Take a photo to remember the shoes and Abby's prayer!"

No Greater Gift (Biblical Story)

Thanks be to God for His indescribable gift! 2 Corinthians 9:15

In Genesis 12, we read about a great man named Abraham. However, the essence of his greatness was not in himself but in his obedience to God. God asked Abraham to leave his family and culture to follow him, not knowing where he was going or what to expect. God also wants us to obey and follow Him.

Later, God offered Abraham a promise: although he was seventy-five years old and his wife was sixty-five, God pledged him a son and to make his descendants as numerous as the stars. Still, Abraham waited, and at age ninety-nine God promised a son again. At age 100, Abraham became the father of Isaac.

Fast forward to Genesis 22. God fulfilled His promise but then gave a different call, a demand so puzzling that Abraham probably felt devastated. He was to go to Mount Moriah and sacrifice his son. What? The command seemed to contradict God's promise.

But wait. As Abraham laid Isaac on the altar and the pile of wood and raised the knife to kill his dear son, God said, "Stop!" God Himself provided a ram in Isaac's place.

We discover in Hebrews 11:19 that Abraham had reasoned that God could raise the dead, and figuratively speaking, he did receive Isaac back from the dead. What joy and peace Abraham must have felt to hug Isaac instead of burying him.

> **Today's Peace Step**
> Reflect on all God has done and is doing in your life to give you peace.

Reading and understanding how God worked in the lives of His people and how He kept His promises helps us trust God. His greatest promise of Jesus gives us our greatest peace. Many years later God sacrificed His only Son, Jesus. He did not stop this sacrifice because we needed it. God had promised time and again that a savior would die for us, and Christ did.

A Grateful Boy

For who has known the mind of the Lord, or who became His counselor? Or who has first given to Him, that it would be paid back to him? For from Him, and through Him, and to Him are all things. To Him be the glory forever. Amen. ROMANS 11:34–36

As we consider God's attributes and abundant grace—as we come to understand that all things come from, through, and to Him—our only response should be gratitude.

Someone has said Christian theology is grace and ethics is gratitude, so it is no accident that both "grace" and "gratitude" are expressed by the Greek word *charis*. A true appreciation of grace will produce gratitude and thanksgiving.

Not long ago Max Lucado told the story of a shoeless street urchin in Rio de Janeiro, Brazil. The small dirty-faced boy, probably no more than six years of age, approached the missionary one day and said, "Pao, Senhor?" (Bread, sir?)

Already headed into a nearby café for coffee, Max motioned for the boy to follow. The child hurried to the pastry counter to select a treat. Then, unlike most beggars who quickly run away, the child paused and ran back. Looking up into the American missionary's face and wearing a smile that would steal any heart, he said, "Obrigado." (Thank you.) Still not satisfied, he then added, "Muito obrigado." (Thank you very much.)

Max said he stood at the coffee bar for a long time. His coffee grew cold, and he was late for his next class. Why? It finally hit him. He said, "If I am so moved by a street orphan who says

> **Today's Peace Step**
> Remember to express gratitude today.

thank you for a piece of bread, how much more is God moved when I pause to thank him—really thank him—for saving my soul!"

Think of a time when someone continued to express gratitude out of a heart that felt thanks. When did you express real thanks?

Making a Difference (Historic Story)

And He was saying to them all, "If anyone wants to come after Me, he must deny himself, take up his cross daily, and follow Me." LUKE 9:23

Heroes walk among us every day, and some give their lives for us. On September 11, 2001, many heroes came forward.

Three people on flight 93 died as they prevented the hijackers from hitting the White House. They thought fast to develop a plan. Todd Beamer, Oracle manager, with the battle cry, "Let's Roll." He and others realized that hijackers had ambushed the plane. He attempted to call his wife, but rerouting ended up with a GTE supervisor and he prayed the Lord's prayer with her, and she overheard Todd plotting to 'jump' the hijackers. The thwarted kidnappers crashed into a field in Pennsylvania, but spared a tragedy in D.C. thanks to Todd, Mark Bingham, Tom Burnett, and Jeremy Glick for using everything they had to storm the cockpit and scare the enemies.

Rick Rescoral, a VP of Morgan Stanley, developed an evacuation plan for the towers and died leading employees down the stairs as he sang, "God Bless America," to encourage and comfort everyone. He is credited with saving 2700 lives. Many police officers also died. They remind us one action can make a difference:

- Firefighter Joseph rescued a woman from an elevator shaft by forming a human chain.
- James Leahy brought in oxygen tanks to rescue people, on his day off.

- Captain Kathy Mazza shot out a window to stop the hysteria that bottle-necked people crowding to escape, giving them another way out. As she carried a woman down steps the tower collapsed on them.

> **Today's Peace Step**
> Be willing to help others without counting the cost.

- Officer John Jergens replied to a radio message to get out "There are people here who need our help."

Living Above

Therefore, if you have been raised with Christ, keep seeking the things that are above, where Christ is, seated at the right hand of God. Set your minds on the things that are above, not on the things that are on earth. COLOSSIANS 3:1–2

While on vacation in New Orleans Bill and Sara stumbled upon an ice cream shop in the heart of the city. They had walked for quite a distance in the heat, so the open door and intriguing smells drew them inside. The thought of something soothing and cold after sweating and walking gave her a sense of joy. As they waited for their turn Sara considered her choices for her favorite or something new and exotic. Then, Sara's eyes were drawn to a sign high above the ice cream area. It read: "Living Above."

Sara quickly assumed this was to notify customers that if no one was present the owner could be found above his shop. Nearby stairs confirmed the obvious. In other words, his life consisted of more than this shop with abandoned bowls, dropped napkins, and maybe even some gum stuck on a wall. Life consists of much more than our work and mundane chores.

The shop owner "lived above" his work. His hopes and dreams and real life were above the level of the day's stress and toil. He might have to work amid clutter, but he could "live above" his circumstances.

> **Today's Peace Step**
> Choose to "live above" the dailiness of life today.

Later, Sara began to think about the lives of Christians. Can we live above earthly possessions and materialism? Can we live above unkindness and self-centeredness? Can we experience a higher purpose than recognition and self-satisfaction? Looking up brings peace as we look above our problems.

Maybe the questions help us begin to comprehend how to *live above* in Christ.

Week 9

Peace Reactions to Struggle and Strife

Prayer During Trials

Gracious Father, we come to you with struggles and strife we face, seeking peace. Appliances and cars break, children cry, and we run out of time. We can feel crushed by careless words and feel angry when someone corrects us or breaks their word. We trust you will work things out for our good and have the best plans for us.

When troubles come and life is hard, help me live above the circumstances. May I run to you knowing that you will comfort and protect me. Exchange my worries for your wisdom, and give me peaceful rest.

With each new trial help me recall how you brought me through a past one and trust you will bring me through the new one. Help me remain calm so I can take things one step at a time. Thanks for always bringing peace in the midst of chaos.

Wisdom from Young Peacemakers

I wait for a while until I'm no longer mad, and then I apologize.

When I'm struggling, I take a break and do something fun.

Inner Peace

"These things I have spoken to you so that in Me you may have peace. In the world you have tribulation, but take courage; I have overcome the world." JOHN 16:33

"A code?" Bob asked.

"Sure, why not?" Sonny answered. "You ask questions, and I'll knock out the answers on the telephone receiver. I'll knock three times for yes and once for no.

Sonny Paterson rapped the receiver.

"Roger. I read you loud and clear," Bob said. "I'll call you Tuesday afternoon around five o'clock. Now, let's pray."

As Bob prayed, Sonny tried to commit his future to God. The flight to Houston would take no longer than the surgery—about three hours. Afterwards, Sonny would be minus a voice box, his communication cut to a knock, nod, tablet, or piece of paper and pencil. Later Sonny might want special laryngeal speech lessons, but for now he wanted the cancer cut away.

"Amen," Sonny replied. "I'll be waiting to hear from you on Tuesday."

> **Today's Peace Step**
> Pray for inner peace.

Sonny Paterson, a prominent businessman and active church layman, had only three more days to talk. How could say everything on his mind? How could he tell his wife and family how much they meant to him? What if he couldn't learn the tricky speech method?

Sonny tried to shut off the negatives. God had never let him down. Sonny also knew that a person's heart can accept something while his mind and body rebel.

Tuesday arrived. Waiting, saying goodbye, rolling to the operating room on a stretcher. Then nothing until waking up with a dry, hollow feeling of something missing. Smiles, hand holding. It was over, the offending cancer removed.

Ring! Ring! Five o'clock.

"Sonny? Bob Strong. Is it over?"

Knock, knock, knock, came the reply.

"Are you in much pain?"

Knock.

"One more question. Have you felt God's peace and grace through all of this?"

There was a pause, and then knocks. Not once, not three times, but repeated groups of three until Bob Strong closed the conversation with another loud "amen."

He Holds the Remedy (Biblical Story)

And all who were sitting in the Council stared at [Stephen], and they saw [Stephen's] face, which was like the face of an angel. ACTS 6:15

After His resurrection Jesus commissioned His disciples to go into all of the world and preach the gospel. Obeying His command, many of His followers were put in prison and others martyred. Some were crucified, beheaded, or stoned. They gave their lives because of their faith in God and heaven.

Stephen, the first martyr, simply waited on tables. He served God so faithfully that God used him to perform great miracles. This caused jealousy among some of the men, and they stirred up the people and elders. Stephen had to stand before the Council as false witnesses lied about him. The high priest questioned Stephen but he turned the questioning as an opportunity to witness to Jesus. His words angered people. As a result, the people stoned Stephen.

Yes, even today men, women, and children are arrested, imprisoned, and killed because of their faith. Religious persecution continues. These people have the faith to stand firm and die for what they believe. Like Stephen in Acts 7, many die with great peace showing in their faces. Stephen, the first martyr, provided a great example of steadfast faith with peace.

> **Today's Peace Step**
> Let your trials build trust. God is molding you to become more like Him.

It's true. Most of us will not endure the hardships just described, but we will, and do, experience trials of various kinds: financial problems, uncertainties, illness, and last of all, death. But wait! Is death really the end? No. In reality it is the beginning!

In his first chapter of his first letter Peter described our hope. He shared how we too would experience the resurrection through which we will live forever. He shares that we can rejoice now because we know what is coming in heaven. We may not see Jesus on earth, but we can believe in the future with him.

Our Shelter

And we know that God causes all things to work together for good to those who love God, to those who are called according to His purpose. ROMANS 8:28

Years ago, a tornado ripped through the Pine Forest neighborhood where Sara lived. She remembers the evening well. Like many folks, she and her family remained glued to the television weather station to decide on the best action plan. They stood in the den right beside the TV when the announcer said, "If you are in the path of this tornado take shelter immediately." At that moment they heard a cracking sound and instinctively ran for the hallway. Bill opened the nearest closet, they stepped inside, closed the door, and—*crash*. One of the tallest pines in their yard suddenly fell through the roof and into the room where they had stood moments before.

Now, everywhere they looked, they saw scattered glass and tree branches on the sofa and throughout the room. They decided to tackle the glass first so they wouldn't step on it and maybe make the situation worst. After that, they began to pick up some of the other mess, but in some ways it seemed hopeless.

Needless to say, Bill and Sara spent most of the night trying to decide whether to go or stay. How much could they do? Who could help?

Although they prayed about it that night and in the days ahead, Sara bemoaned the situation and whined about the cost and clean-up. She asked herself, "Do we have the time? Do we have the money?" As it turned out, God provided both.

It took Bill and Sara a while to see their situation from God's perspective. Later, she thought of this: we had been struck down, but not destroyed (2 Corinthians 4:9). God used their trouble to make them stronger in their faith. She realized He was, and is, our shelter in this and every storm.

> **Today's Peace Step**
> Look back and realize how God used your past troubles for your good.

Seeing the Light (Historic Story)

Look unto me, and be ye saved, all the ends of the earth: for I am God, and there is none else. ISAIAH 45:22 (KJV)

Due to a heavy snowstorm on January 6, 1850, a teenage boy was unable to attend his usual church service. He did, however, make it to a primitive Methodist chapel where a layman was substituting for the absent pastor. The man was ill-equipped for the task, but his text was Isaiah 45:22.

He then added, "A person need not go to college to learn to look. Anyone can look—even a child can look." Since this layman knew little else to say, he kept repeating the Scripture verse, and a certain young man did look. This teenager had been unhappy and under conviction for many months, and about that time, the speaker pointed to him and said, "Young man, you look miserable. Young man, look to Jesus Christ!"

Well, by faith the young man did look and by the power of the Holy Spirit was converted. Although he had no formal education he later became astute in theology and was Victorian England's best known Baptist minister. He even preached at the Metropolitan Tabernacle with a seating capacity of 8,000 people. He was known for his rich command of language, clear voice, and dramatic ability to attract crowds.

In 1867 he founded Stockwell Orphanage for boys and one for girls in 1879. He also founded a charitable organization that distributed food and clothing for the poor. The man who once knew no peace even published a sermon series titled "The God of Peace."

> **Today's Peace Step**
> If you haven't already, look to Jesus and your darkness will become light. Look to Jesus and find peace!

Who was this miserable young man who was once admonished to look to Jesus and be saved? He was the well-known and beloved Charles Haddon Spurgeon.

Staying Calm

Do not fear, for I am with you; Do not be afraid, for I am your God. I will strengthen you, I will also help you, I will also uphold you with My righteous right hand. ISAIAH 41:10

Let's take a moment to consider some of the major stressors in our lives and some possible solutions. Let's consider ways to live what we believe.

1. *Listening to the news.* Every day we hear about major disasters, health issues, addictions, sex trafficking, and more. The possibilities of more problems may cause discouragement. Solutions: Limit your exposure to the news. Pray for the people and situations discussed. Memorize and then recall Bible verses to help you keep your focus on Christ. This will help you exchange those worries with God's wisdom.

2. *Reliving past mistakes and sins.* This is a major ploy of Satan. He will try to pull you down and even lie to you regarding your forgiveness in Christ. Solutions: Remind yourself of your former confession and remember as Scripture states, "Resist the devil, and he will flee from you. Come close to God and He will come close to you" (James 4:7–8). Believe God forgives you. Memorize 1 John 1:9 that states He forgives us.

3. *Playing "what if" with the future.* What if these plans don't work out? What if an illness overtakes someone in the family? What if there are financial issues? And on it goes. Solution: Remember your faith and all of God's promises. After all, Romans 8:28 reminds us that God works everything out for our good if we love and serve Him.

These are a few ways to lean on God and let go of worries to find inner peace. These are steps that many

Christians live. The steps provide a way to change our thinking and habits so that we react with trust first and not worry.

> **Today's Peace Step**
> Start your day with prayer. Stay in touch with God all day.

Week 10

Peace and Rest

Prayer for Rest That Restores You

God and Father, you created and control all things, and I desire to honor you in all I say and do. My thoughts are too often focused on self and circumstances. Sometimes it seems as though the whole world is in chaos and confusion, and I know my heart is often in unrest. I want peace that lets me rest calmly.

Remind me today of Christ's words in John 8:12, "I am the light of the world. Whoever follows me will never walk in darkness, but will have the light of life" (NIV).

As I follow you, I do not have to fear darkness of night or any dark thoughts that pop in my mind, for you will enlighten me. Give me the courage to trust in you when I react with fear or feel confused by news I hear.

Let me sleep in peace as I trust you to be in control. Let my rest restore and refresh me.

Wisdom from Young Peacemakers

I need an angel in my ear so I can remember to be good, and then Mommy will have peace.

When I'm scared, I hug my big bear.

Lessons from a Skunk

But if we walk in the Light as He Himself is in the Light, we have fellowship with one another, and the blood of Jesus His Son cleanses us from all sin. 1 JOHN 1:7

Believe it or not, the skunk is an intelligent creature. In fact, his method of ridding himself of fleas is ingenious.

First, he fills his mouth with straw or grass and wades into a stream. With only his muzzle visible, the skunk appears to have a bushy mustache. The fleas, in fear for their lives, move upward to get out of the water. Soon the stalks are black with hundreds of the insects, so the skunk simply opens his mouth, releasing the mustache, and the uninvited guests float downstream.

I wonder. Do we hate our sins as much as a skunk hates his fleas? Do they bother us like the sting of fleas biting the skunk? If so, we can be sure that God provides a remedy. God forgives us when we ask, but we still must resist falling back into old patterns. One of our problems is a lack of trust in our Savior. We become anxious and fearful. We listen to the temptation of Satan and words of unbelievers that cause us to choose to sin. Then we lose our peace as we know we sinned. Or we feel guilty and don't believe we are forgiven. If you are like me, you want to be rid of these pesky sins as much as the skunk wants to be rid of his fleas.

> **Today's Peace Step**
> Confession renews our relationship with Jesus Christ and will bring us peace and rest!

Think of it like this: As the skunk's fleas cannot survive in the water, our fearful thoughts and anxieties cannot survive when we trust God and let go of them as the skunk lets go of the straw. This, of course, includes spending time with Him in prayer, Bible study, and confession of sin.

A Sudden Storm (Biblical Story)

He caused the storm to be still, So that the waves of the sea were hushed. PSALM 107:29

One day after performing miracles and teaching in parables Jesus told His disciples to get into a boat to go to the other side of the lake. They quickly obeyed him and set out.

Not long into the trip and with little warning, a violent storm erupted, and water began to sweep over the boat. Dark clouds, strong winds, and a sinking boat that filled with water filled them with fear. Terrified, the disciples ran to Jesus but found Him sleeping. Yes, He had often told them not to worry, but this seemed different and, because it involved their own lives, difficult, if not impossible.

"Lord, save us," they cried. "We're going to drown!" Jesus was not ignoring them but giving them an opportunity to trust Him instead of letting fear fill them.

Luke 8:24 says, "He got up and rebuked the wind and the raging waters; the storm subsided, and all was calm" (NIV). Blue skies, balmy breeze, and still water replaced the storm. Jesus showed His friends His power and that He is God the Son. If He made the wind and the waves, surely He could control and conquer them. At this point, Jesus asked his friends, "Where is your faith?"

We don't hear an answer from the disciples, only a question to each other. In fear and amazement, they ask each other, "Who is this? He commands even the winds and the water, and they obey him."

The question "Where is your faith?" remains for us to answer. Whenever we don't feel peace, whenever we face a challenge or feel overwhelmed, as though we will drown in our problems, the question remains. Those are the moments to pause and pray for strength and for God to increase your faith. Choose to remain calm, and know He is with you.

> **Today's Peace Step**
>
> When you feel afraid, respond to "Where is your faith?" with trust in Jesus.

Fear and a Flashlight

Then Jesus again spoke to them, saying, "I am the Light of the world; the one who follows Me will not walk in the darkness, but will have the Light of life." JOHN 8:12

Think back to your childhood for a moment. Were you afraid of the dark? Dr. Howard Chapman, a minister in Marion, Iowa, admits to his fear of the darkness as a young boy. Chapman's parents served as missionaries in Sierra Leone, West Africa, at the time, and he reports that no one walked anywhere at night without their trusty flashlight.

They lived in an area with no streetlights. You needed a flashlight to keep from stumbling and falling. Another problem? Poisonous snakes hunted at night. If a cobra or a black mamba bit you, you would be dead within minutes.

At about five or six years old, Chapman recalls walking along a dark path with his mother. Wanting something to do, he begged her to let him carry the flashlight. She finally agreed but reminded him the flashlight was not a toy. "We need to be careful of snakes," she said.

"Her words freaked me out," Chapman admitted. "I started to shine the light into the long grass and bushes on the trail."

After a few minutes, she snatched the flashlight away and asked, "What do you think you're doing?"

"Looking for snakes," he answered.

"No," she replied. "We are not looking for snakes. It's more important to look at the path ahead. If we see something, we stop. A snake will be afraid of the light and slither into the dark. Then we can safely move on. The light, however, must always shine on the path ahead of us."

Today's Peace Step

As we reflect on Scriptures, let God's light shine before us to guide our path, and our fears will flee away.

It's true. When our path seems dark, we are not to turn and stare into the problem, terrified by what may be lurking there. We have Jesus, the light of the world, to look at.

The Truce (Historic Story)

"Stop striving and know that I am God; I will be exalted among the nations, I will be exalted on the earth." PSALM *46:10*

It was a cold, clear night. The trenches stretched for 100 miles from Germany through Belgium and France. It was Christmas Eve 1914, early in World War I. The area was called No Man's Land, and that's exactly how it felt for Graham Williams, a British soldier on guard duty.

As Williams gazed toward the German lines he later wrote, "I was thinking what a different sort of Christmas Eve this was from any I had experienced in the past. . . . Then suddenly lights began to appear along the German parapet, which were evidently make-shift Christmas trees, adorned with lighted candles, which burnt steadily in the still, frosty air!"

As Williams and his men watched, more trees appeared and then came a shout, "You no shoot. We no shoot!" Then a German soldier stepped into No Man's Land and, likely in a smooth tenor voice, began to sing "Stille Nacht, Heilige Nacht."

> **Today's Peace Step**
> If you sometimes feel the whole world is in confusion and chaos, choose to recite a Bible verse or sing a hymn that reminds you of God's faithfulness.

Feeling the warmth and beauty of the carol, the British then sang "The First Noel," and so it continued into the night. Clapping. Handshaking. Even exchanging gifts across the line.

Williams wrote, "I thought this was a most extraordinary thing—two nations now singing and enjoying each other's company in the middle of a war."

Time magazine later stated that more than 100,000 men participated in the brief and spontaneous cease-fire that spread up and down the Western Front in the first year of World War I. The truce symbolized peace on earth and goodwill toward men that is often lacking not just on the battlefield but in our lives every day.

A Powerful Name

"These signs will accompany those who have believed: in My name they will cast out demons, they will speak with new tongues; they will pick up serpents, and if they drink any deadly poison, it will not harm them; they will lay hands on the sick, and they will recover." MARK 16:17–18

Years ago, a friend sent Sara an unusual gift. When she first unwrapped the package she was confused. It seemed to make no sense. This red and white needlepoint was a 2- by 8-inch object, but what was it? Sara read her note that went something like this: "I know. You must look intently to see the significance, but once you see, it will remain forever."

She looked. Yes, if you focused just right on the one word, then the message became obvious. It was "Jesus." It was a type of optical illusion. Once she saw the real word, she always saw it.

Most of us are familiar with phrases like, "I'll back you up," "I've got your back," or "I've got you covered." No doubt we say these words with good intentions to support our friends, but the word *Jesus* is all we need to recall. He always remains loyal. The very name should bring us peace.

Far more reassuring than anything we might promise a friend, Jesus is always faithful and always ready to help us. His name is powerful enough to use to heal and protect people. Believers can use the name Jesus to help others.

> ### Today's Peace Step
> Let the name of Jesus be one to honor in your home and use to help others find peace, hope, and help.

Today, the Jesus needlepoint still hangs over the doorway between Sara's kitchen and den. It reminds her of the constant presence, protection, and intercession of our Lord. It's also a reminder that, as believers, we can pray in the name of Jesus to help others and to give us the peace in knowing the power of His name.

Week 11

Blessed with Peace

Prayer For God's Blessing of Peace

Dear Lord, thanks for giving me peace that passes under-standing. Your Word reminds me that I will face troubles, but I should not worry, for You are with me. I will rejoice when you bless me with peaceful days filled with blue skies. Help me recall my blessings that also bring peace. As I remember past prayer answers and times you kept me safe, I will feel more confident that those thoughts will give me peace as I trust this day to You.

Troubles may make headlines, but your Word is full of greater news of eternal life and love. Your promises are reminders that You are with me, you care for me, and you give me your peace. I can wake up each morning with a smile and thank you for the day You made because I trust in You.

Wisdom from Young Peacemakers

I sit down and do something I love.

Mommy hugs me, and Daddy makes me laugh. Then I feel loved.

Moved with Peace

"See, I have placed the land before you; go in and take possession of the land which the Lord swore to give to your fathers, to Abraham, to Isaac, and to Jacob, and their descendants after them.' Deuteronomy 1:8

Military orders meant a move to Miami. Karen could not sleep. Her mind filled with thoughts of drugs and gangs. She knelt and asked God to protect their four growing children and the unborn son within her. She reflected on familiar Bible passages of God's protection of Abraham and Joshua as well as Peter and Paul. She prayed for hours and finally paused and listened to God.

She simply heard, "I am with you always" and "Let your heart not be troubled." Peace filled her heart, and she slept soundly. She shared her prayer time with her husband, and they thanked God together. They moved to Miami with no worries for their children and lived there for fifteen years. The children never turned to drugs or made other poor choices. Sunshine and cool breezes made life pleasant. The children thrived and started to enter adulthood during those days with good career choices. The older children met and married wonderful spouses.

> **Today's Peace Step**
> When anxious, pray and listen until God gives you inner peace.

They had struggles with great damage from a major hurricane, a few lightning strikes including one that cracked water pipes, and months of unemployment after Jim's retirement, but God brought them through it all.

Her husband testified as an expert witness regarding drug cases on ships during his tour of duty. Only after his retirement did he let Karen know that drug cartels had a $20,000 hit out on him. The Coast Guard inspected his car at work daily, and he parked it in the garage at night. She had not known about the hit, so she had not worried. Sometimes we pray until we have peace, and other times God keeps us from knowing about danger while He protects us.

God Uses Gideon to Bring Peace (Biblical Story)

Then Gideon built an altar there to the LORD and named it The LORD is Peace. To this day it is still in Ophrah of the Abiezrites. JUDGES 6:24

Gideon hid in a winepress trying to use his own power to thresh wheat to separate the chaff. That's hard work, usually done with wind power in ancient times. Gideon used a wooden flail to pound the grain. This was a stick with a chain and a swinging shorter stick attached to beat the grain. His low self-esteem made it hard to believe when God chose him and sent an angel who called him a valiant warrior.

Gideon tested the angel's messenger with a fleece, not once but twice, and then presented an offering on a rock, which the angel consumed with fire that sprang from the rock. Gideon accepted God's call to battle the Midianites.

He built an altar and named it Jehovah-shalom, which means "the LORD is Peace." The name reflected the trust he had in God's ability. He never wavered in his obedience as he achieved victory for his country.

Then God tested Gideon by whittling down the army. First the fearful ones—22,000 of them—left. Then they drank water at a stream or river, and God chose those who lapped it like a dog while holding a weapon, which left a mere 300 men to face thousands. That was enough for an almighty God. God gave Gideon wisdom to use the noise of clay jugs and the light of torches to win a battle without a fight. This emboldened the Israelites to pursue and defeat the Midianites. Archeologists have uncovered fragments of a clay jug with the inscription *Jerubbaal*, an alternative name for Gideon.

> **Today's Peace Step**
> Obey God and follow His call even when you don't think you are capable.

Gideon's obedience in battle resulted in forty years of peace for Israel. He made mistakes and opened the door for idolatry in the land, but Hebrews 11, called the hall of fame, praises Gideon's faithfulness.

Photo Albums

Remember His wonderful deeds which He has done, His marvels and the judgments from His mouth. 1 CHRONICLES 16:12

As a child Karen's dad loved taking photos and filling albums with black and white pictures. As an adult he snapped colorful photos. He filled a trunk with albums and continued photographing their lives. She wondered if these albums mattered because they remained hidden away.

After her mother passed away, she visited Dad and noticed he had replaced her clutter of trinkets with the albums of photos. He shared about his wonderful childhood in spite of the Great Depression and lack of money, how God brought the country and him through World War II, and how God blessed many people. He said that gave him joy every day.

They laughed at pictures of her brothers and she splashing in water, stuck in three-foot-deep snowdrifts, baptisms, vacations, and ones of her dad as a boy. He told stories about the three of them as babies. He also shared photos of his grandparents and stories of him raising turkeys. He had planned to sell his biggest turkey and buy something special for himself but instead used the thirty-plus-pound bird for the family gathering. That was a great party and more memorable than any toy or gadget.

When Dad ended up in the hospital with terminal lung problems, Karen created a digital display of some of his favorite photos. She'd play them when he seemed restless. He looked at them and calmed down. When his brother visited, they talked about memories from each photo and smile or laugh, and it eased her uncle's worry of losing his brother. After her

> **Today's Peace Step**
> Snap or view a photo so you can rejoice over memories now or later.

dad passed, her older brother and she digitized all the photos. The memories gave Dad peace and joy. Remembering the joys of our past as well as joys of Bible stories can bring us peace.

Princess Pocahontas (Historic Story)

So, Abram said to Lot, "Please let there be no strife between you and me, nor between my herdsmen and your herdsmen, for we are relatives!" GENESIS 13:8

According to a letter written by Captain John Smith, Pocahontas saved his life: "After some six weeks fatting amongst those Savage Courtiers, at the minute of my execution, she hazarded [or risked] the beating out of her own brains to save mine, and not only that, but so prevailed with her father, that I was safely conducted to Jamestown."

Many people have heard of the rescue. Some historians think she actually acted out a part her father assigned her. Pocahontas means "playful one." Captain Smith wrote that her wit and spirit stood out. Like a curious and playful child, she liked to visit the village of the settlers, but she also served as a peacemaker. As a member of the Powhatan tribe, she always came with a group from her tribe and shared how they lived on the land. The settlers traded tools for food and also exchanged young men to learn one another's cultures and language.

At one time Pocahontas came to Smith during the night with a warning of a plot to kill them. She refused any reward since showing up with English items could jeopardize her life. Another time when Henry Spelman, on an exchange to her tribe, ran off to join a friendlier tribe, but was caught and she interceded and saved his life. Her father moved the tribe further west to discourage his daughter and avoid the English, who needed more food than the tribe could give during a very harsh drought. Alas, Captain Samuel Argall stole her in hopes of exchanging her to free captured Englishmen. He changed his mind and let her go, but she remained in Jamestown, where John Rolfe fell in love with her and married her.

> **Today's Peace Step**
> Be willing to be a bridge to help people live in peace.

With her help, John succeeded in growing tobacco on the land, and that saved their town. She was baptized, although whether it was of her own will or forced remains debatable. She helped bless the settlers with peace and served as a bridge between her tribe and the settlers.

Heartfelt Peace by Linda Gilden

And the peace of God, which surpasses all comprehension, will guard your hearts and minds in Christ Jesus. PHILIPPIANS 4:7

Usually a very safe driver, Gerald raced through downtown. Sandra, his wife, held her abdomen trying to diminish the pain that stabbed harder every time they hit a pothole.

When they arrived at the emergency room, Sandra was immediately wheeled back to an exam room, where doctors began tests to see what was causing the pain. Three days later, after emergency surgery, Sandra woke up in the intensive care unit barely aware of what was going on.

Each day Sandra learned more about what had happened. She lay in bed with tubes coming from many places in her body.

After a few days, Sandra felt better but spent very little time talking to God. Sandra always thought if she ever was in a life-threatening situation, she would find herself pleading with God to heal her. But as she recovered, Sandra realized that other than listening to praise music, she had very few thoughts of having a conversation with God. Eventually, Sandra mind filled with questions for God: *Where are you, God? How did I end up in such a serious situation? Can you not say something that will make me aware of your presence? Why don't my thoughts go straight to you?* *I seem to just be lying here all day every day.*

> **Today's Peace Step**
> Continue to deepen your relationship with God so His peace surrounds you in difficult situations.

After almost two weeks in the hospital, Sandra's focus changed. Instead of worrying about God speaking to her, she began to thank Him that during the entire hospital stay she never felt anxious or apprehensive. She felt peace. Instead of talking to Him, Sandra was filled with His gentle peace. Instead of using her energy to talk, she rested in God's presence.

When in a crisis do you panic and search for God, or do you spend your time resting in His presence?

PEACE IN RELATIONSHIPS

We know if we really want to love, we must learn to forgive. Forgive and ask to be forgiven; excuse rather than accuse. Reconciliation begins first, not with others but ourselves. It starts with having a clean heart within. A clean heart is able to see God in others. We must radiate God's love.—MOTHER TERESA, THE JOY IN LOVING

Once we have inner peace and choose to live in peace, it is easier to have peace in our relationships. We cannot change others or make them calm, but we can pray for God to do that. We can choose to respond in peace, with love in our hearts.

Week 12

Peace with Mindfulness and Joy

A Prayer for Understanding

Lord, you gave King Solomon a wise and understanding heart to rule a great nation. Please give me a little understanding each day to manage my children, home, work, and outside activities. It's so easy to come to conclusions too quickly and find I've based my decisions on false assumptions. Help me pause and listen well, prayerfully seek your wisdom, and act with understanding.

Help me turn from selfishness and look to you for guidance instead of simply wanting things done my way. Let me see into my child's heart to understand his or her feelings and thoughts. Let me be understanding of the people in my life to know how to respond to their needs. Let me pause before I speak to really understand the other person. With understanding, it's easier for peace to reign.

Wisdom from Young Peacemakers

If Mom is stressed, I ask if I can do anything to help.

My sisters and I clean the house when my mom looks too tired and sounds grumpy.

Grandmother's Gifts

I am giving you a new commandment, that you love one another; just as I have loved you, that you also love one another. JOHN 13:34

Sara's grandmother Belle was not a wealthy woman, but she managed to give Sara some remarkable gifts and memories. When Sara was seven and learned to play "Rock of Ages" on the piano, Grandma Belle explained how the Lord was her support and helper in all of her decisions and even in her trials. She shared that God is like a strong rock, and as Sara observed her, she wanted God for her rock too.

Grandmother must have known she wouldn't live to see Sara grow up, because one day she handed Sara two large silver coins and said, "I wish I could offer you more, but keep these silver dollars to remember me by." She also liked to bring marbles when she came to visit. Sara can still remember rolling those marbles around on her bedspread and dividing them into the various colors. Today, a clear vase filled with Grandmother's marbles adorns Sarah's kitchen windowsill. Another time Grandmother said, "Someday you will be married. Ask God to show you the man who will seek to love you the way God loves you!"

> **Today's Peace Step**
> Whether you have a spouse or not, seek to love others the way God loves you.

Grandmother died when Sara was only eight. Due to her age, she wasn't allowed to attend the funeral, but she remembers spending the time walking through her friend's garden singing "Rock of Ages." She promised herself she would remember her grandma's advice about a future husband.

Decades later, Sara still finds great delight in the man who fulfills her Grandmother Belle's advice. In fact, she just thought about it as Bill applied a special ointment to her aching back. Yes, she truly believes this man seeks to love her as God loves her. What joy and peace!

Steadfast Devotion and Joy (Biblical Story)

Rejoice in the Lord always; again I will say, rejoice! Let your gentle spirit be known to all people. The Lord is near. PHILIPPIANS *4:4–5*

Who is one of the most mentioned women in the New Testament? Yes, it's Mary Magdalene, who appears in all four Gospels. From a town called Magdala on the western shore of the Sea of Galilee, Mary Magdalene was one of several women who helped support Jesus' ministry.

In the beginning, Mary's background was not an impressive one. In fact, at one point seven demons possessed her. However, Jesus completely changed her life when He delivered her from seven demons. It was deliverance to devotion! Here are some examples of her devotion.

Others fled, but Mary stood by Jesus as He suffered and died on the cross. She saw Him buried and planned to later anoint Him with spices. When she returned to the tomb on the third day Mary felt dismayed to see the stone over the entrance rolled away. Mary ran to share the news with Peter and John, who then dashed to the tomb and confirmed His body was indeed missing. They left, but Mary stayed at the tomb. Mary, weeping, looked in the tomb and saw two angels. They asked her why she wept, and she said, "Because they took away the Lord." Her despair and unrest kept her searching.

> **Today's Peace Step**
> Be joyful and thankful that God has risen and knows your name too.

She talked with a person she thought was the gardener, and asked where he had moved the body of Jesus. Jesus simply said, "Mary!" He astonished her, and she filled completely with awareness and joy. Yes, honored to be the first-person Jesus appeared to after His resurrection, she was also the first to announce, "I have seen the Lord!" (John 20:18). Peace replaced her tears and searching once she saw Jesus, the risen Lord.

Finding Calm

So then, my beloved, just as you have always obeyed, not as in my presence only, but now much more in my absence, work out your salvation with fear and trembling. PHILIPPIANS 2:12

You know your day will be an adventure when you wake up without hot water and heat; have a neighbor tell you boards are falling off your fence in the backyard just when you are attempting to send the plumber an email about a leaky toilet, drop your glasses in an awkward spot and can't retrieve them because of hip surgery, find a sticker for an overdue safety inspection on the electric panel, and have to shoo your dog from a strange cat coming into the yard through the new hole in the fence . . . all before 9 a.m.

Stephanie Parker McKean, Sara's author friend from Scotland, recently posted those words, but within twenty-four hours, she also posted this message from a friend: "You have done a great job raising Luke in the Lord, and the fruits are ripening. May you always have comfort in that and celebrate Luke's life as you celebrate your birthday and continue with your wonderful books!" She chose to dwell on her friend's words rather than her words of her misadventures.

Luke, a Marine major, served several tours in Iraq and Afghanistan and also flew a World War II Focke-Wulf airplane. One day, while piloting to a memorial service for one of his men,

> **Today's Peace Step**
> Ask God to direct your thinking today and guide you to encourage someone else.

his plane went down. Stephanie said he flew straight from his plane into the arms of Jesus. Luke is remembered by his men as one who never drank or used profanity. Luke read his Bible daily and used God's wisdom to advise his Marines. He is buried in Arlington National Cemetery. She chose to dwell on how Luke served the Lord rather than her loss.

A Vigil for Life (Historic Story)

Greater love has no one than this, that a person will lay down his life for his friends. JOHN 15:13

Eve Gordon was a young nursing student in London just before World War II. One Saturday as she did her rounds with a doctor they approached the bed of a young man suffering with pneumonia. The doctor told Eve that he would probably not make it through the night. Later in the evening, while sitting by his bedside, Eve realized he had overheard the doctor and begged her not to leave him. Early on Sunday morning church bells began to ring, and the patient survived the night. He also survived the war.

When war broke out Eve served in France and was later evacuated from Dunkirk along with over 300,000 other evacuees. The Secret Service tapped her to serve. One night Eve parachuted into France with lots of radio equipment under her coat and orders to set it up. The Germans made a random check of whole blocks. They caught Eve and took her into a house, where a soldier hit her in the head with a rifle butt, knocking her to the floor. Later, opening her eyes, Eve saw a pair of shiny jack boots. This officer stood over her and reached for his pistol.

> **Today's Peace Step**
> Build hope into someone's life, and give God the praise.

Eve silently spoke to God, saying, "Lord, let it be quick!"

The next thing she knew the officer reached for his handkerchief, wiped the blood from her head, and said, "You may go!" Eve stared at the man.

Suddenly Eve realized she knew this man. Yes, he was the one who had suffered with pneumonia, and she had sat by his bedside all night. Some might consider it a coincidence, but Eve knew God arranged it all. He placed them together both times. Once she gave the man hope, and once he gave her hope. Those are God-incidents.

Golden Slippers

Now there are varieties of gifts, but the same Spirit. And there are varieties of ministries, and the same Lord. 1 Cor-
INTHIANS *12:4–5*

For the umpteenth time Sara lifted her gold metallic shoes from their box and chuckled. Purchased for half-price during a family vacation years ago, she thought she had found a prize. *Surely,* she thought, *my fuzzy and practical bedroom shoes back home are no match for these braided rhinestone beauties.*

Many miles and days later, she examined her golden slippers again. No marks. No scratches. No mates? Ready to slip them on and be a lady of leisure, she noticed one shoe fit snugly across the top of her foot while the other was a thong, with a small strap to fit between the toes. She immediately reached up to the closet shelf for the familiar fuzzy slippers that had always served so well. Suddenly, they were not only warm but wonderful. Oh, what comfort! In the days and weeks that followed the cozy slippers were her constant companions—almost like a good friend. She stopped and thanked God for them.

Sometimes our choices in our Christian life are like the purchase of those gold shoes. Anxious to look good and carry our weight, we have accepted jobs without asking God if it is His choice. Too late, we realize the shoes don't fit. They are mismatched for our feet. We need to take Paul's remark to heart: "We have different gifts, according to the grace given us" (Romans 12:6, NIV).

For years Sara kept those two flashy shoes in a dusty box. Yet somehow they served a purpose. The golden slippers reminded her not only to laugh at her bloopers, but to examine her gifts to see if all decisions match up to His perfect will for her.

Today's Peace Step

Ask God to increase your joy as He shows you His plan for today and for all of your future.

Week 13

Peace through Forgiveness and Acceptance

Prayer for Complete Forgiveness

Dear Lord, it's hard to forgive when I'm still hurting. I know you forgave me for all I've ever done wrong, so help me to forgive anyone who hurts me. You forgave the soldiers and others who abused and killed you, so help me forgive those who have caused so much pain.

Help me accept the changes in my life over which I have no control. The new normal has been difficult and hard to navigate. Let me focus on my blessings and what I have, to be content and grateful. I have so much, starting with your love. I am blessed with a home, family, and friends. I am blessed with creation and beauty you created. Thank you for this day you made. Help me bless someone else and bring comfort to someone who is hurting.

Wisdom from Young Peacemakers

Forgiveness helps me put my anger in the garbage.

Forgiveness gives us a new chance to be friends.

The New Normal by Joan Patterson

This is what the LORD says, He who makes a way through the sea and a path through the mighty waters. ISAIAH 43:16

A new phrase has arisen from the uncertainty caused by the pandemic: "the new normal." Speculative plans are made not knowing if changes in the pandemic will cancel it. No one knows what the future holds, but the topic weighs on the minds of both young and old.

Joan's new normal began about three years after her diagnosis of multiple sclerosis. Joan managed her symptoms until one fateful day when she went to take a step and almost fell on her face. Her right foot worked the way it had for forty years. Her left foot no longer lifted when she brought it forward. Walking became a concentrated effort.

That eventful day at her job as a teacher she had exerted so much energy dragging her foot around that home and bed sounded inviting, but she was in charge of an evening event. It required a dressy outfit including high-heeled shoes. Her husband implored her to change shoes after watching her stumble around clinging to display tables.

She said, "I can't change shoes. I need to make a good impression for my students and the businesses in attendance."

"You're not making a good impression by almost falling," he replied.

She retreated to the back room; sat on a chair; removed her beloved high-heeled shoes, her sign of femininity; and tenderly placed them in their box. Tears clouded her vision and wet her cheeks. A part of her died.

A brace from her toes to the back of her knee held her foot in place. No pretty shoes could fit over it.

Joan chose to accept her new normal and be happy rather than sulk and mourn her previous life. The loss of strength, the ability to walk, and dependence was her future. She reminded herself daily to appreciate what she could still do on God's new path for her.

> **Today's Peace Step**
> Accept changes that come, and thank God for what you have.

Prodigal Son Reconciled (Biblical Story)

So he set out and came to his father. But when he was still a long way off, his father saw him and felt compassion for him, and ran and embraced him and kissed him. LUKE 15:20

A father watched his son leave home after he asked for his share of the inheritance. That meant, "Dad, to me you are dead, and I want the money I would inherit." This dad probably watched every day for his son to return and prayed for him as he watched. One day, the father saw him returning and ran to meet him and hug him.

Prodigal means "wastefully extravagant," or "reckless". His father could only hope for his son to return, knowing his son had made some poor choices.

The son lived his own life apart from his dad, spending money on drinking and carousing. Once he had spent all his money he realized he had no true friends, no one who would support him emotionally or give him a meal and shelter. The swine that wallowed in mud ate better than he did, and appeared happier. He had no training or job reference and found the lowliest job around of feeding squealing pigs who greedily ate their slop. It depicted his life as a prodigal.

The Bible says he came to his senses. That means he stopped being foolish and irrational. Sometimes in a dispute one person—sometimes both people—behave foolishly. Letting go of pride and admitting you made a mistake takes courage and humility, but that's what opens doors to reconciliation. Continual prayer is the other key ingredient.

> **Today's Peace Step**
> Prepare your heart to restore a relationship with forgiveness and love.

One person can leave and break a relationship, but it takes two hearts that are ready to reconcile for a happy reunion. The father had not heard his son's rehearsed confession but already chose to show love. They both came together to make peace and restore the relationship. The son chose to return as a servant. The father chose to celebrate the return with a party and gifts.

Stay in the Right Lane!

Do not neglect doing good and sharing, for with such sacrifices God is pleased. HEBREWS 13:16

Suzy seethed when her friend got the promotion she wanted. She hardly spoke to Chloe for a week. She tended to grumble when someone bought a new car, wore new clothes, or even got a meal that looked better than what she ordered. She had a hard time focusing on her work because she always watched other people and compared herself to them.

The next morning Chloe gave Suzy sweet-scented pink roses from her garden and said, "I know you also wanted this job, and I'm praying God will bless you this week."

Suzy mumbled, "Thanks." That evening she received an unexpected large check in the mail from a family member. She told Chloe the next morning and received a big hug and smile.

Chloe added, "I'm so happy for you. Do you have plans on how to spend it?"

Suzy asked, "I'll probably get a new car. How can you be happy for me?"

Chloe replied, "I like seeing how God blesses people. It's a good choice to replace your old car. What type of car will you choose? What color?" Suzy described her dream car.

Suzy thought about Chloe's reactions and realized she always felt jealous. Chloe often gave her little gifts like sharing a dessert, flowers from her garden, and encouraging words. Suzy never gave gifts to anyone. Suzy asked Chloe how she could be happy and not jealous.

> **Today's Peace Step**
> Rejoice when God blesses someone else.

Chloe replied, "I try to stay in my own lane and never compare how God blesses others to what He does for me. He knows what is best for each person. I thank Him for my blessings, so gratitude fills my heart. I like to do what God does, and that's blessing people."

Suzy resolved to compare less and be thankful, and she accepted Chloe's invitation to church.

Dr. Martin Luther King Jr. (Historic Story)

Let justice roll out like waters, and righteousness like an ever-flowing stream. Amos 5:24

Dr. Martin Luther King Jr. spoke out for justice and quoted from the prophet Amos. Amos voiced rage at the injustice within the northern kingdom of Israel. He denounced the people who celebrated the feasts lavishly while letting the poor suffer. Justice involves righting wrongs in society such as unequal treatment of people and the abortion of innocent babies. His faith inspired his desire for nonviolent activism such as marches and peaceful demonstrations.

Dr. King, educated in Black schools during segregation, spoke out to follow the route of nonviolence to bring social reform for marginalized groups. He understood that hatred burdens our souls and said, "Hatred paralyzes life; love releases it. Hatred confuses life; love harmonizes it. Hatred darkens life; love illuminates it." He knew that love could drive out hatred. He believed conflicts should be settled peacefully. It broke his heart to see discrimination and senseless deaths such as bombings. He pressed on even when outsiders committed violent acts against peaceful protesters, bombings of Black churches, and murder of anyone.

People responded when Dr. King depicted the way to fight poverty, stating: "True compassion is more than flinging a coin to a beggar. It comes to see that an edifice which produces beggars needs restructuring." He looked at the larger picture of how to change society and pull people out of poverty by creating new circumstances and better opportunities.

Dr. King chose to shed light on the darkness of poverty and discrimination with hope, dreams, and ideas that would bring lasting change.

> **Today's Peace Step**
> Be willing to illuminate the darkness and bring changes that help people.

As a man and preacher, he understood God's forgiveness. He preached that all people might put aside differences and learn to reach out in loving kindness. Humility and love as Christ lived could lead to greatness.

Freed Heart That Forgave

"And forgive us our sins, For we ourselves also forgive everyone who is indebted to us. And do not lead us into temptation." LUKE 11:4

Two people faced the same problem. Someone stabbed their child, one victim a teen, the other victim a grown man with daughters. The man who lost a son tried to continue saying the Lord's Prayer every day but could not get past the words reminding him to forgive. How could he forgive? Yet God asked him to forgive. Jesus on the cross asked His Father to forgive those who killed him, God the Father's only son. Day after day, the dad asked for help to forgive and be free from the anger.

The woman who lost a teen sat in self-pity mourning her son. She kept reading Matthew 18:23–25 about a man forgiven of a great debt who turned around and had no mercy on someone who owed him a tiny debt. She knew God forgave her everything and began praying to forgive the murderer.

They both felt imprisoned in pain, anger, and grief. When the father sat in the courtroom before sentencing, he finally felt compassion for this man who had no family supporting him, who needed forgiveness and a new start. At the end of session, he held out his hand and said, "I forgive you." They correspond, and the father has shown love and grace to the man. Since then, God has refreshed the father, and he continually recalls the good times and sees his son as a young boy playing and spending time together or as a dad with his girls. The memories bring smiles and laughter.

> **Today's Peace Step**
> Ask God's help to forgive, and choose to do it.

The woman and her husband chose to forgive. Her choice released her to experience joy again and live for her other sons, grandchildren, and family. The witness to others of remarkable forgiveness continues to change many hearts after they experience unimaginable sorrow.

Week 14

Peace in Relationships

Prayer for Peace in Our Relationships

I am grateful for the people in my life and ask you to help me see and encourage the best in each one. Let me not be critical, but help me find reasons to praise each individual.

Holy Father, I praise and thank you for the picture you provide of a Christian marriage. For those of us who are couples, may we seek to fulfill the example of Christ's love for the church and the church's submission to Christ. May we stand together in joy and sorrow. May we also know that you walk beside us all the way.

For those of us who are not married, may we build a strong support system and wholesome relationships. May we be grateful for our families, including our church families. Bless us as we reach out to make new friends and welcome new members into our families.

Wisdom from Young Peacemakers

I need to know someone a bit before I can become a friend.

To get along with others, tell the truth.

A Profound Mystery

So husbands also ought to love their own wives as their own bodies. He who loves his own wife loves himself; for no one ever hated his own flesh, but nourishes and cherishes it, just as Christ also does the church, because we are parts of His body. EPHESIANS 5:28–30

Did we leave something out? Yes. Verse 32 in the NIV reads: "However, each one of you also must love his wife as he loves himself, and the wife must respect her husband." Loving leadership. This is God's call for the Christian husband. A wife's call: submission and respect.

The word *submit* is from the Greek word *hupotasso*. It comes from the word *hupo*, which means "under," and *tasso*, which means "to arrange in an orderly manner." There are several different interpretations of the word including "to identify with" and "be in support of." It does not mean subjugation or slavery.

Now, Sara's husband might be embarrassed here, but she will take the risk. Here is a man who constantly puts her first. Over the years she remembered those little surprises like an Uncle Wiggly rabbit figure for the backyard and an old milk crate to hold a certain plant. Mundane? What about a phone call ending with, "You sound tired. Why don't I take you out for dinner?"

Over and over again, Sara sees her husband's compassion and self-sacrifice. Yes, he loves his wife as he loves himself. Sara? Well, she feels she has a long way to go with Christ-like love. However, her heart has developed a tender appreciation and great respect for her spouse's character.

In this passage Paul reminds readers of the sacrifice the Triune God made when the Son, who is equal with the Father, became man and offered his life in order to save us. Having adopted us into the family of God, he shared that our marriages should reflect the

Today's Peace Step
Be thankful for all the ways your spouse shows love.

love Christ has for the church (the husband's role), and in return, the church should offer back loving submission and respect (the wife's role).

Mary and Joseph (Biblical Story)

And Mary said, "Behold, the Lord's bond-servant; may it be done to me according to your word." And the angel departed from her. LUKE 1:38

What sudden and shocking news astounded Mary? Although pledged (engaged) to a man named Joseph, the angel Gabriel told her she was going to give birth by the Holy Spirit to the Son of God, and He would be given "the throne of his father David." This declared this baby to be the long-awaited savior the prophets had shared about. The angel told Mary to name Him Jesus and that this God/man would reign over the house of Jacob forever. His kingdom would never end.

Although Mary's heart and mind may have pondered numerous questions, she accepted the angel's explanation and responded with, "I am the Lord's servant. May it be to me as you have said."

In Matthew 1, we read about Joseph's reaction to the news of Mary's pregnancy. Likely dismayed and disappointed, Joseph was a godly man and planned to protect her from shame. Then, through a dream, God sent an angel, who told Joseph to not be afraid. The angel explained that this child, whom Joseph was to name Jesus, was the Messiah who would save his people from their sins. This fulfilled the prophecies that a virgin would bear a child whose name means "God with us."

> **Today's Peace Step**
>
> Continue to live up to the vows and promises made when you married, because faithfulness helps bring peace.

Without further hesitation Joseph took Mary as his wife but had no union with her before she delivered Jesus. God gave them the unity of both understanding the wonder of this special baby. It all took place just as the prophets had proclaimed centuries earlier. He chose to honor God and Mary in his marriage.

Laughter is Important

A joyful heart is good medicine, but a broken spirit dries up the bones. PROVERBS 17:22

It all began when Jim, a once confirmed bachelor, decided it was time to propose to Nancy, his longtime girlfriend. On this particular day Nancy was helping him with chores on his outdoor property. Out of the blue, Jim said, "Nancy, will you go to the shed and bring me those hedge clippers on the table?"

Wondering why he didn't retrieve them himself, Nancy headed for the shed. She spotted the clippers easily but also saw a small box she couldn't resist. Inside, Nancy found a beautiful engagement ring, which she tucked in her pocket. Trying not to react, she handed him the clippers and waited.

"Well, what is the answer?" Jim asked.

Then, not to be outdone and wanting a formal proposal, Nancy smiled and answered, "Well, what is the question?" He made a more formal proposal, and when she said, "Yes," he slipped the ring onto her finger. Jim and Nancy have celebrated many years together and continue to laugh and enjoy their love.

A happy couple at the same church shares stories about their early years. One night on a date Deb turned to Carol and said, "Say, why don't we drive over to Mississippi and get married?"

> **Today's Peace Step**
> Loosen up.
> Laughter is good
> for relationships.

Carol's answer: "Deb, you know I can't do that. Mama said I had to be home by ten."

Sara, married for many years, shares that recently, cuddled with her husband, she said, "You know what? You are a gem!"

Bill grinned and replied, "No, my name is Bill. Be careful. It's too soon for dementia." They burst into laughter.

Tears Also Speak (Historic Story)

And I give them eternal life, and they will never perish; and no one will snatch them out of My hand. JOHN 10:28

Like Job in the Old Testament, tragedy came to Horatio and Anna Spafford more than once. First their four-year-old son suddenly died of scarlet fever. Then a year later, in October 1871, a horrific fire devastated downtown Chicago that killed about three hundred people, left around 100,000 homeless, and destroyed Spafford's sizeable real estate investment north of Chicago. Although many of Horatio's properties were destroyed, the Spafford couple sought to display Christ's love by helping others in need.

Two years later Spafford decided his family needed a holiday in England. Delayed due to business, he sent his wife and four remaining children ahead. However, on November 22, 1873, their vessel was hit by an iron sailing ship, and 226 people were killed, including his four daughters. Floating unconscious on a plank, Anna survived, arrived in South Wales, and sent a telegram to her husband stating, "Saved alone."

Spafford set off at once to be reunited with Anna. During his voyage the captain summoned him to the bridge and showed him the very spot where the ship sank and where his daughters had died. He wrote to Rachel, his wife's half-sister, "On Thursday last we passed over the spot where

> **Today's Peace Step**
> We cannot see into the future, but we can know that God holds us in his hands and keeps our souls safe.

she went down, in mid-ocean, the waters three miles deep. But I do not think of our dear ones there. They are safe, folded, the dear lambs." According to the story, Spafford returned to his cabin and wrote the beloved hymn, "It Is Well with My Soul."

Extended Stay

I will ask the Father, and He will give you another Helper, so that He may be with you forever; the Helper is the Spirit of truth, whom the world cannot receive, because it does not see Him or know Him; but you know Him because He remains with you and will be in you. JOHN 14:16–17 NIV

Well, it finally happened. Water flowed everywhere. Overflowing washing machine and a broken toilet. Sara and Bill loved their country home, they had no other choice. It was time to connect to city water. However, more problems lay ahead.

They needed to line up a plumber and an electrician and decide which side of the driveway to dig up. They had unanswered problems to solve. Who would keep the dog? When and where would they move? What would they pack?

Well, you get the drift. Other problems arose that meant Sara talking to the plumber and electrician while Bill worked, as well as trying to operate from an Extended Stay hotel. Finally, after five days in their temporary location, they moved back home only to be told they must move again due to unexpected complications.

On the first morning back at home Sara found this note on the counter after Bill left for work. It simply stated, "I love our Extended Stay!"

Though still groggy, she smiled. Yes, their marriage and love remained an "extended stay." They were committed and continued to find peace in the midst of troubles.

She read further in John 14, to verse 23, which states, "If anyone loves me, he will obey my teaching. My Father will love him, and we will come to him and make our home with him." There could be no better "extended stay." Her mind immediately jumped to God's words. It's true, she told herself. God lives in the hearts of His children, and the promise is forever.

> **Today's Peace Step**
> Reflect on this:
> God has promised
> to abide with
> you forever!

Week 15

Peace in the Home

Prayer for Family Peace

Dear Father, Bless our home, and help us be united in purpose and hearts. Help me be forgiving and loving always, willing to extend mercy and grace balanced with training my children. Help me model peace.

Help me humbly admit mistakes and ask forgiveness of my family. Help us create a warm and inviting atmosphere where children can bring their friends to play and study. Help us maintain order to make life easier.

May we be respectful and use good conflict resolution skills when we disagree. Help us choose peaceful solutions. May we love one another and hold fast to our biblical values. Let peace reign on our home.

Wisdom from Young Peacemakers

A husband should tell his wife she looks good even if she has no makeup on and her hair is a mess.

A man needs a wife who can clean up after him. A wife needs a man who can pay the bills. They also need to pray together. Then they'll be happy.

Mom says we'll have peace when I obey the rules. She sure gets mad when I don't.

Honoring One Another

Honor your father and mother (which is the first command-ment with a promise). EPHESIANS 6:2

Love came to visit her son and his family with five chil-dren. She discovered her son had run over her middle grandson, Jamie's, bicycle that Jamie left in the driveway. His mom suggested Jamie save money to buy a second hand one. Out shopping that day, Love couldn't resist buy-ing him a new bicycle. Then she worried the others might be jealous. Amazed that they cheered for Jamie and peace still reigned, she couldn't resist buying each child a gift. Love's son knew they were not perfect, but they worked at having peace at home.

The five children sometimes expressed anger at a parent like, "I hate you," "You're mean," or "My friend's mom (or dad) says it's okay." They heard the response, "You're talking about someone I love very much. God gave me a wonderful spouse, and it hurts me when you say mean words about her (or him)." Mom and Dad both supported the other parent. If one disagreed with what the other did, they privately discussed an idea to improve his or her actions next time. When one parent asked their child's forgiveness, they both hugged and praised the child.

Honoring one another so children would honor them as parents began with the marriage. They studied Ephe-sians 6 and chose to honor and respect one another. They promised not to disrespect each other to friends, family, or children. It was not easy when out with friends who shared the funny things their spouses did. They shared more positive thoughts.

Amazingly, honoring one another kept peace in the home and encouraged the children to be kinder to all members of the family. Coming together daily to pray included praying a simple one-sentence prayer

Today's Peace Step
Choose to honor family members and pray together.

thanking God for the person sitting to the left. Praying for a sibling or parent helped the children consider their needs and joys, made them more empathetic, and cut out yelling, teasing, and mean words.

Timothy's Home (Biblical Story)

I am reminded of your sincere faith, which first lived in your grandmother Lois and in your mother Eunice and, I am persuaded, now lives in you also. 2 TIMOTHY 1:5 (NIV)

Imagine a young enthusiastic teen being chosen as Paul's traveling companion. Paul also wrote that Timothy was like a son to him. Paul often sent Timothy to preach and share the way of the Lord. Paul praised Timothy for his faith and attributed it to his home life and upbringing. That's a high compliment for a family. Imagine his mother and grandmother sharing faith over meals and at bedtime plus answering all Timothy's questions as a child. His father would have helped him learn Greek and promoted his education. That cherished childhood made Timothy an eager disciple of Paul and gave him the courage to serve God.

The son of a Greek father and Jewish mother who lived in Lystra, Timothy ministered to at least five churches. He recognized the truth regarding salvation when he first heard about Jesus (2 Timothy 3:15). That's a man who developed a deep faith and learned to think for himself. Paul's first trip to Lystra, a town of superstitious and uneducated people except for the Greek-educated Hellenes, ended in the people stoning him. The second journey ended with Timothy joining forces with Paul and stretching Timothy's faith to become a church leader.

Archeologists discovered inscriptions on a large stone and coins that identify Lystra and its location in the Roman province of Galatia. The town is in the modern country of Turkey.

> **Today's Peace Step**
> Share faith with children.

Timothy, from a small, insignificant village, became a great missionary. His mother and grandmother created a home where they educated Timothy and instilled a strong faith in him. The home is where faith begins and grows when parents intentionally share faith. Shared faith fosters a peaceful and thriving home where children feel free to follow a career of their choice.

Family Meetings

In their hearts humans plan their course, but the LORD establishes their steps. PROVERBS 16:9

"Time for a family meeting!" Dad called everyone to the table. Bowls of popcorn and fruit placed in the center invited the children to fill a plate before discussions began.

"The first item is how we can have peace and stop the teasing and arguing." The kids presented ideas and decided they'd put a quarter in a jar every time they broke the peace. If they made kind jokes that didn't hurt someone's feelings that would be fine.

They chose family activities and dates. They also decided each one could invite a friend for the game night. Then Mom brought out letters and appeals for donations from different organizations.

Dad said, "Mom and I tithe money for church and other regular giving, but we thought it would be fun to have you decide where to give some extra money we set aside." He stated the total amount.

They read and discussed each appeal, from local shelters and sport teams to campaigns to feed the hungry. They decided how to give and who would answer the letters.

Then Dad asked each one to share anything on their mind they wanted improved or anything about which they were thankful.

> **Today's Peace Step**
> Schedule family meetings to maintain peace and add fun in the home.

James shared that he didn't like a sibling just taking his things without permission, and everyone agreed to remember to ask. Darlene expressed happiness about meals and devotions.

Mom said, "Thanks. It's a lot of work cooking for our family. I want more help with meals and want you all to learn to cook." Dad and all the kids agreed to help and chose dates to cook.

Before the meeting ended one of the boys kicked someone under the table and one of the girls teased one of her brothers, so they had to put money in the jar. Then they discussed what to do with the grumble money. They decided they needed to find a way to give it to a place of joy.

Eric Liddell, Family Man of Faith (Historic Story)

Therefore the LORD God of Israel declares, "I did indeed say that your house and the house of your father should walk before Me forever"; but now the LORD declares, "Far be it from Me—for those who honor Me I will honor, and those who despise Me will be insignificant." 1 SAMUEL 2:30

Eric Liddell won the gold medal in the 1924 Olympics while clutching a paper in his hand. The few words on the paper simply stated, "1 Samuel 2:30." Eric's life reflected his honoring God, including his refusal to run the heat for the 100-meter race because it was scheduled to take place on a Sunday, the Lord's Day. He qualified for the 400- and 200-meter races and won medals in both, plus broke the world record in the 400-meter race. He spent that Sunday worshipping God.

Eric Liddell never basked in fame for his athletic ability. Eric, born in China as the son of a missionary family, followed his parents' example. He focused on God's call to serve in China as a missionary and cared for his family. He married a woman from Canada who served in China alongside him. At the time when he took a break to visit family in Scotland, on furlough, he had two children. His daughter Patricia, six at the time, recalls enjoying her time with cousins and grandparents in Edinburgh.

They sailed back to China in a convoy of ships during World War II. Enemies torpedoed some of the ships. A torpedo struck their ship but never detonated. They arrived in China, but because it had become more dangerous to live there, Eric sent his pregnant wife and two children to Canada. He died in China in 1945, when Patricia was merely ten. At the internment camp run by the Japanese in China, Eric, who looked out for everyone's welfare, convinced the camp directors to allow exercise and set up fitness programs.

> **Today's Peace Step**
> Live your faith
> so that it will be
> your legacy.

Although so young, Eric's wife kept his memory alive for their children. They grew up knowing their dad's faith and his commitment to serving others. He left a legacy they carried on.

Moving with Peace

"The LORD is the one who goes ahead of you; He will be with you. He will not desert you or abandon you. Do not fear and do not be dismayed." DEUTERONOMY 31:8

Darlene and her husband prayed about moving. They had offers in another state for Frank to work but no offers where they lived. They had the money to cover the move, but they would be uprooting their five children from family and friends.

After days of prayer, they felt peace about it all. They took one trip to find a house to rent. They found a spacious home with a yard and a tree to climb in a nice neighborhood. It had room for schooling and sleeping for all.

They made moving plans, including leaving the three oldest children with Darlene's mom to homeschool them and the two younger ones with Frank's parents. They rented a moving van and knew they'd have to make a few trips. On the first trip, they picked up Darlene's brother to help. It was much more work and expensive than expected. Darlene's mom gifted them with unpackers on the second trip. They needed that!

It took a month to move, and even then they still had boxes to unpack. Everyone helped unpack the truckloads of items.

> **Today's Peace Step**
> Before a major change, pray and pray-pare to face unexpected challenges.

The children liked the home and area. It took a while to make friends, and a few set up weekly Zoom calls with old friends. It took months to choose a church and find the right homeschool group to join. They chose the ones where they had made friends.

Julia, the youngest child, started making friends with neighbors. One older couple taught her gardening, and she nurtured her own little plant.

Week 16

Peace through United Purpose

Prayer For Unity

Dear Father, help us be united in purpose. Let us focus on the people we serve who need us and not our own desires. Let us not be concerned about whether we are noticed or appreciated.

Unity begins with our attitudes, so please keep our hearts pure and full of love. You give us purpose, sometimes for family and sometimes for serving the world. May you guide us in how to serve and love all those involved.

Help us to respond with love when we face unexpected emergencies or crisis. Let us build strong bonds knowing that you are the one who unites us.

Wisdom from Young Peacemakers

I like helping people.

Our family makes sandwiches for the homeless. I add heart stickers to the baggies.

Disaster Recovery

God is our refuge and strength, a very ready help in trouble.
PSALM 46:1

After a category-four hurricane devastated their area of the Florida Keys, Rebecca manned phones at the church her husband pastored, and helped where she could. When a company asked where they could bring an eighteen-wheeler full of work boots to donate, she directed them to the church parking lot. She went to the local park where a restaurant was feeding the hungry for free and announced the news of free boots with the details of when to come. Within minutes of the truck parking, the driver distributed all the boots. Rebecca facilitated other aid as well.

Within a week, an organization that helped with disaster relief, having heard of Rebecca's great work, approached her and asked if she'd work for them. After praying with her husband, she took the job and quickly was promoted to lead case manager because of how she continually found answers to help victims and her development of a good tracking system.

> **Today's Peace Step**
> Offer help when you hear of a disaster.

She worked with churches all over the country who called to offer help, and matched up needs with offers. She discovered that no one would allow their money to be used to replace damaged appliances on houseboats not covered by insurance. After more prayer, a large organization offered $25,000. They were happy to partner to help people in houseboats.

A week later the organization called again to say no other church in her area would accept their money, and they believed her church was so united in purpose to serve anyone in need they'd like to offer another $25,000. Again, she directed it to something no one else would cover.

Rebecca's team attended all local meetings at community centers, churches, mayor's meetings, and more. They coordinated assistance. People heard about her team's work and came. They felt peace and relief knowing someone listened and wanted to help.

Syntyche and Euodia (Biblical Story)

I urge Euodia and I urge Syntyche to live in harmony in the Lord. PHILIPPIANS 4:2

In chapter 4 of Philippians Paul focused on contentment and harmony but started off with a mysterious note that these two women, Euodia and Syntyche, should live in harmony. Paul asked his companion to help the two. He recalled how the women worked with him in the cause of the gospel. He knew disunity disrupts ministry and the work God calls us to do. These words flow into ones that call us to rejoice and not be anxious. He called for prayer and giving requests to God, and knew that results in peace that transcends understanding. It's hard when we see great Christian workers, churches, and ministries, split due to differences, pride, or stubbornness.

Paul then urged readers to think about what is true and commendable. Dwelling on the positive lifts our focus off ourselves to something of more value. He ended with the encouragement that the God of peace will be with them when they practice those ideas.

What great thoughts on attaining peace! The women's names mean "fortunate" or "blessed" and "good journey." They each experienced different situations, but Paul called for them to be of the same mind and purpose even if one seems very blessed and the other appears to be on a hard journey. He wanted them to focus on God's will and not their desires or winning in a situation. We should remember that our ministry is all about God and His call. We've all faced differences. It's fine to debate and consider alternative plans, but after prayer we need to realize God's will and choose unity. Forgiveness and mercy need to be extended to restore relationships and harmony. We should live in harmony, as part of the family of God.

> **Today's Peace Step**
> When you are at a crossroads, pray for God's will and peace.

Paul wrote this while in prison in dire circumstance. He later mentioned that he had learned to be content with little or much. His secret was leaning on strength through Christ. It's the right perspective that we look beyond ourselves and look to God.

Peace through Coffee by Britt Mooney

Take my yoke upon you and learn from me, for I am gentle and humble in heart, and you will find rest for your souls.
MATTHEW 11:30 (NIV)

Jesus said we would have problems and spoke of rest not as an absence of a burden, like vacations, but trading our worry for His easy yoke. What does all this mean?

Several years ago, a church-planting network, Phoenix Community of Atlanta, started a coffee company to raise money for missions and relief in the United States and around the world. (You can read more about it in the book *Say Yes: How God-Sized Dreams Take Flight*, by Britt Mooney.) Churches across the country, regardless of denomination, race, or doctrine, used these products.

Those church fellowships found themselves unified by two things: first, the love of amazing coffee, and second, and most importantly, saying yes to following God to bring relief through the gospel.

Britt and his wife were successful teachers but gave that up when God called them to missions in South Korea through the coffee company, a radical change that began a path of wonder and adventure they wouldn't trade for anything.

Jesus gave His peace the night before His crucifixion, a peace despite His imminent horrific experience. His peace was different, "not as the world gives, do I give to you" (John 14:27).

> **Today's Peace Step**
> Examine the ways you are participating in God's purposes and listening to His Spirit for direction.

How do we get such inner peace? Britt and his wife found it through intimacy and purpose. The peace of Christ isn't inactivity. It's active, living, purposeful. His original twelve disciples were a rough group of dudes. What kept them together? Following Jesus who led them in purpose.

People can't separate God from His purposes. He seeks to reconcile all creation back to Himself through the Son. Followers must participate. There are great promises for those who love Jesus (intimacy) and say yes to whatever He asks (purpose). Romans 8:28 reminds us that *all* things will work for good. Not some. *All*. God's purpose gives people unity and peace through trusting Him to work out problems.

Christmas for the Soldiers (Historic Story)

In everything I showed you that by working hard in this way you must help the weak and remember the words of the Lord Jesus, that He Himself said, "It is more blessed to give than to receive." ACTS 20:35

In 1918 Christmas preparations began in July, before Germany surrendered in World War I. The YMCA, Red Cross, and other organizations carried out a massive campaign to surprise American troops and French people. Newspapers in the States kept the secret, only disclosing details on December 22.

On Christmas Day, all 1,500 YMCA huts in Europe displayed decorated Christmas trees, held festive caroling and church services, and passed out Christmas boxes to every soldier, about two million men. Volunteers at each hut dressed up as Santa and distributed gifts to French children everywhere. Soldiers gave toys and candies to millions of French children. Wounded serviceman in hospitals also enjoyed entertainment. They each woke to find a bright red stocking hanging at the end of his cot, filled with candy, a pocketknife, and other comforts. Every YMCA location performed a comedy sketch, written for the men, and drew lots of laughter.

In Montigny, a little French village of 600 people, with gray stone homes and red tiled roofs, the people enjoyed a special treat. President and Mrs. Wilson celebrated Christmas there with the 26th Infantry Division. They also visited the army headquarters in Chaumont.

At home the news of peace and Christmas for the soldiers, marines, and sailors lifted spirits. Christmas Eve began with hymns and carols sung in Madison Square and other squares, all decorated with Christmas trees. People crowded into churches the next morning, heard messages of peace and hope, applauded men as soldiers of the Prince of Peace. Many concluded with singing "The Star-Spangled Banner." The War Camp Community Service distributed 10,000 stockings with clothing, candy, and theater tickets to soldiers who landed in New York. Restaurants, theaters, clubs, and families hosted men, provided meals, and gave them gifts.

> **Today's Peace Step**
> Be a blessing to someone in need.

United through All the Days We Have

Make my joy complete by being of the same mind, maintaining the same love, united in spirit, intent on one purpose.
PHILIPPIANS *2:2*

Karen and Jim phoned their five children and shared the sad news that he would start hospice care at home that day. His time on earth was limited. They wanted the children to see him as often as they desired in the coming weeks, so they offered to pay any airfare. That allowed everyone to say goodbye and share any last words. They took turns coming as they had over the past few years of the battle with cancer. At one point, three of them came together.

They came to serve. They all wanted their dad to be comfortable and happy. They laughed when the workman had to create a longer hospital bed to fit their dad's six-foot-four-inch length.

They cooked for their mom, sat with their dad, and cared for his needs. They helped him walk, get to the bathroom, and sit on a couch. Rebecca, the oldest, shared memories of camping, tea parties, and other favorite childhood activities. When Jim's brother Luke came, the children listened to their dad and uncle share stories from the past. The boys shared jokes, and Darlene sang and created a recording of her singing her dad's favorite hymns. After she left, whenever Jim got restless, turning on Darlene's recording made Jim smile and relax. Jim had always enjoyed family, and he rejoiced with the visit of each child.

> **Today's Peace Step**
> When a loved one is ill or dying, choose to serve and share happy memories.

Other people stopped by to visit Jim, filling the days with voices of people he loved and prayers with many. After

Jim passed, the children took care of the arrangements. Rebecca's husband, a pastor, performed the service. They all shared ways they would be helping Karen with Jim's things and her future plans.

Week 17

Peace through Kindness

Prayer to Be Kinder

Dear Lord, help me think before I speak and choose kind words. May the Holy Spirit control my tongue rather than my emotions. Help me to see the image of you in each person so I might speak with love. Let me be thankful for the blessings you send each person. Even if someone irritates me, let me forgive and respond with kindness. Let me be understanding that hurting people reach out in anger as a cry for help, a cry for a little kindness.

Help me be kind in my actions, even small ones, to bless others and lift their spirits. May I sprinkle joy into their lives.

Thanks for the people in my life who always speak kindly and encourage me. They have blessed me and lifted me up when I'm down. Let their example remind me to bless others, especially those with pain in their hearts. May I spread kindness into lives to bring peace.

Wisdom from Young Peacemakers

I help pick up things so the house is cleaner. That helps us relax and feel peace around us.

Kindness makes people happier.

Walter and the Coach

Be of the same mind toward one another; do not be haughty in mind, but associate with the lowly. Do not be wise in your own estimation. ROMANS 12:16

Coach J. returned home from baseball tryouts. He asked his daughter, "Do you know Walter?" He described him and gave his last name.

"Sure, he sits by me in history class."

"Other coaches think he's a big problem, but he's a great player."

"Well, kids tease him, but he's nice to me. I think that because he's a little slow in school and so big, they make fun of him and try to get him in trouble. I bet he'd be fine on your team. You're always fair and make peace between the players."

Coach J. picked Walter. At the first practice someone started yelling, "Fatso is up."

> **Today's Peace Step**
> Praise someone who other people tease or put down.

Coach J. stopped the practice. He said, "We're a team, and that means praising players and not teasing them. I think Walter is the best hitter of everyone and a great catcher. Watch what he does at practice." Walter stepped up to bat and hit a slammer. He caught all the pitcher's throws.

The next day Coach J.'s daughter said, "Dad, you must have made the team respect Walter 'cause the boys were sure nice to him today and didn't let anyone tease him.

He grinned and looked even taller. He said you're the best coach ever and he's glad to be on your team."

Her dad replied, "I just gave the team a pep talk and reminded them that I believe everyone has talents, including Walter. I asked them all to be kind. He sure can hit and catch!"

That season the players all stuck together, praised each other, and won almost every game. Walter also did better in school, and one of his teammates became a study buddy to help him. Other coaches mentioned that the team seemed to have a spirit of peace and kindness.

The Kindness of Obed and Ruth (Biblical Story)

And at mealtime Boaz said to her, "Come here, that you may eat of the bread and dip your piece of bread in the vinegar." So she sat beside the reapers; and he served her roasted grain, and she ate and was satisfied and had some left. RUTH 2:14

Two of the kindest people in the Bible became husband and wife. Boaz noticed the widow Ruth gleaning wheat in his field. She picked up the leftover grain that the harvesters missed.

Boaz encouraged her to continue to glean in his fields and assured her that he told his men not to harm her. Then he asked her to share lunch with him. She asked why he favored her. He explained that he had heard how kind she treated her mother-in-law, Naomi. He knew she was a Moabite, a nationality of enemies to the Jews, yet he shared his bread with her. Moab was the nation that refused to share bread with the Israelites. He blessed her with what her ancestors withheld. He also had his workers drop extra grain for her to pick up.

Naomi praised Boaz's kindness. Naomi urged Ruth to stay in his fields as Boaz had asked her, until the harvest ended. At the end of the harvest, the men would be winnowing barley on the threshing floor. Naomi asked Ruth to go secretly, lie down by his feet, and ask Boaz to spread his garment over her. This symbolized a marriage proposal from Ruth.

Boaz reacted with admiration and remarked that her desire to marry him, an older man, revealed her best kindness. He gifted her with six measures of barley. Boaz met with another relative labeled guardian-redeemer. This man had first choice to redeem Naomi's land, which would mean he had to marry Ruth. The other kinsman declined, and Boaz followed the custom of giving one of his sandals to the man to seal the decision. Boaz married Naomi, and she gave birth to Obed. She became an ancestor of King David and Jesus.

> **Today's Peace Step**
> Be kind. Kindness inspires lasting relationships.

Seeking True Kindness

What is desirable in a person is his kindness, And it is better to be a poor person than a liar. PROVERBS *19:22*

Patsy asked Kathy, "Have you seen Suzy's artwork? She creates beautiful macrame."

"No," Kathy replied. "We've met up in the craft department at stores and chat about what we make when the children play at the park, but I've never seen her work. I should invite her over since we both like making things and our children are friends."

"You mean you've never been to her house and seen her work?" Patsy asked.

"No. I don't even know where she lives. She's sweet, and our husbands serve together."

Patsy called Suzy and confirmed that Kathy had never visited. Then she phoned several friends who had been together when their friend Amy shared how Kathy banged on Suzy's door and barged in to yell at her for not joining a certain group. Patsy had spoken to Kathy since she had found the rumor hard to believe of her friend who was in Bible study with her. She was so upset that Amy had tried to ruin Kathy's reputation that she set up a meeting at Amy's home.

Patsy invited Kathy to the meeting and even drove her. Once there, she confronted Amy in front of their group of friends. Amy denied everything and asked them to leave.

In the driveway Kathy said she appreciated Patsy defending her. She said that maybe Amy had a problem

> **Today's Peace Step**
> Seek the truth when
> you hear a rumor
> to keep peace
> among friends.

with confabulation or exaggerated and changed facts. She said she had called Suzy to invite her to join a group, but

Suzy said she could not add another activity. She had wondered if some of her friends had avoided her but thought maybe they were simply busy. Suzy responded that she remembered that call, but Kathy had been very sweet and understood. They had not spoken about it again, and she would like to know Kathy better.

Gladys Aylward (Historic Story)

But how are they to preach unless they are sent? Just as it is written: "How beautiful are the feet of those who bring good news of good things!" ROMANS 10:15

Gladys gasped when she looked around the streets in China. She grew up feeling that God made a mistake making her so short and dark haired while her friends were blond and tall. In China she looked much more like the people around her. She struggled to become a missionary but finally found a way to go to China as an assistant to Jeannie Lawson, a missionary in China.

Once together, Jeannie and Gladys opened an inn to serve people and share their faith with visitors. The Chinese people did not trust foreigners, so Gladys ran out when she heard a mule team on the road grabbed the harness, and led the lead mule to the inn. The other mules followed expecting food and received it. The two women provided good food, beds, and stories about Jesus to the drivers.

The Mandarin of Yangchen, the local leader, sought her help during a prison riot because she claimed that trusting God meant having no fear. She calmed the prisoners and suggested the Mandarin leader relieve the prisoner's boredom and provide jobs to pay for food.

The Mandarin leader wanted Gladys to help stop the practice of foot binding. She accepted the challenge because it gave her access to local people. She opened her heart and then her doors to take in starving orphans. When they had to flee from Japanese attackers they trekked toward Sian. At the Yellow River no one

Today's Peace Step
Trust God to lead you to help others.

would help them cross, so they sang songs and prayed. Their voices attracted a Chinese patrol, who brought them across where they then reached an orphanage in Sian. The growth of communism forced her to return to England in 1947, but she moved to Taiwan in 1970 to establish a new orphanage. The Chinese called her The Virtuous One for her tireless work to help others.

Tears, Not Words, Encouraged a Heart

Those who sow in tears shall harvest with joyful shouting. PSALM 126:5

One evangelist, Dr. T., met weekly with an atheist. He argued and defended his faith to no avail. He shared his faith and reasons for believing in Christ, but his friend countered every point he made.

He did not want to give up and felt he could not succeed with other people if he did not succeed with this friend. He spent hours praying, searching Scriptures, and reading books by great theologians. Every week he drew up a new debate and met his friend at a coffee house. They remained at peace and friends, but Dr. T. had no peace in his heart or mind. He could not rest due to his concern for his friend's soul. After many months of meeting, he met his friend and simply wept. The friend asked why he shed tears, and he explained that he cared so much for this friend that he could not bear his going to hell for his unbelief. Dr. T. expressed his great love for his friend. He said he'd be there the following week.

That next week his friend shared that he finally believed and asked Dr. T. to pray with him. Dr. T. wanted to know what changed his mind. His friend replied that his tears moved his heart and opened it to God. He had not known that anyone cared so much, and it gave him a glimpse of God's love for him. Once he accepted God's love, his heart filled with a peace he had never known.

> **Today's Peace Step**
> Love someone enough to cry for his or her soul. That's love that brings peace and change.

Dr. T. realized that he needed to truly love someone enough to cry for their soul if he wanted to change lives. His tears expressed more kindness than his words ever did and made it easier to share the love and peace of Christ with others. He went on to change many lives.

Week 18

Peace through Conflict Resolution

Prayer to Resolve Problems

Dear Lord, you are the Prince of Peace. Help me resolve conflicts peacefully without heated arguments or grudges. May I understand the point of view of others and know their words reveal their emotions about the issues. Help me calmly share my perspective. May I follow your example of asking questions when I am confronted. Give me wisdom to come up with possible solutions that can work.

Within my family help us to pray and understand one another before making decisions. Guide us to choose the best solution to try. May we agree to accept the decisions made. When we cannot agree let us be willing to love one another and realize we have different views.

Fill my heart with peace in the midst of conflicts, that I may love all those involved.

Wisdom from Young Peacemakers

If trouble comes up I might say, "Let's think about it and talk later."

If my sister would always let me have my way, we would not fight.

You can say the same thing nicely.

Changing Conflicted Hearts

All bitterness, wrath, anger, clamor, and slander must be removed from you, along with all malice. EPHESIANS 4:31

Sean took his wife and her sisters out for lunch. The conversation as usual turned to animosity toward their youngest brother, the executor of their late mother's estate. Sean planned to negotiate peace with them, and after complimenting the three for their beauty, he asked them each the same questions. Each time they all nodded, "Yes."

"You were asked to be the executor and turned it down. Is that correct?"

"You knew your other brother's health prevented him from being executor. Is that correct?"

"That left Teddy, who grew up with learning problems and poor grades. Is that right?"

Then he pointed out the current problem with another question: "So is it his fault that he made a poor choice of what lawyer to hire and cannot get things done in time?" They all shook their heads no. A few mentioned some senseless things he did as a child and his hard time passing on to each grade. Sean shared about his love of life, great cooking, and sense of humor.

> **Today's Peace Step**
> Admit your part in any conflict, and communicate on progress and changes.

Sean said, "So we all need to forgive him, support him, and see if he'll let any of you help him, or perhaps let me ask to help him."

They smiled and said, "Oh, Sean, would you offer to help him?" They agreed it was their own choices that resulted in their brother being made executor, so he was really not to blame. He agreed to help and would keep them informed, but they had to agree not to be angry with their brother any longer. They all nodded, Sean made some jokes, and they enjoyed the lunch.

Sean stopped to see Teddy and chat. He offered to review the papers and help with the work. Teddy was glad for the assistance. Sean kept everyone informed of the estate's progress.

Miriam's Jealousy (Biblical Story)

While they were at Hazeroth, Miriam and Aaron criticized Moses because he had married a Cushite woman. NUMBERS *12:1 (NLT)*

The siblings of Moses complained about his ministry and his marriage to an Ethiopian, a black woman. Jealousy and pride apparently crept into Miriam and Aaron's hearts.

Miriam had danced and sung when God used her brother to free them from slavery in Egypt. She praised God for parting the sea and hurling Pharaoh's horses and riders into the sea. Now, she challenged God's choice of Moses as the leader. Naming Miriam first indicated that she was the instigator of the criticism.

Aaron, the older brother, stood beside his brother because Moses wanted a helper to speak for him. God used Aaron and made him the high priest. Aaron had some authority to question problems and make sure people observed all the laws, but lacked authority to question Moses' authority.

As a result, God called the three siblings to the Tabernacle. He spoke to them privately. This kept Miriam and Aaron from being publicly disgraced or humiliated. God did not criticize either of them, but instead confirmed his choice of Moses to speak face to face with Him. When God departed and the cloud moved away, Miriam stood there with leprous skin. Aaron cried out in repentance. Then Moses cried for God to heal his sister. God answered the brother's prayers but had Miriam banished from the camp for seven days. The only reaction from Moses was a statement of his humility. Moses' humble attitude kept him from reacting with hurt or anger.

> **Today's Peace Step**
> Ask God to resolve conflicts, especially within your family.

Later, in Numbers 17, we find God reaffirming Aaron as His choice for priest. Moses and Aaron continued to work together, and Moses never showed any animosity about his siblings' criticism.

God stepped in to resolve the conflict. The brothers' prayers revealed their love for their sister. Love and prayer are the glue that helps us remain close even after conflicts.

Pumping Up Peace by Pam Farrel

There is an appointed time for everything. And there is a time for every matter under heaven. ECCLESIASTES 3:1

Ever find your marriage in a stalemate? Bill and Pam Farrel are known for their relationship ministry, Love-Wise.

Does this mean their relationship is conflict free? No, peace has to be built up, like muscles strengthen by lifting weights with daily reps.

Bill had just transitioned from a full-time pastoral role at a megachurch. He loved that job, but he loved speaking with Pam on marriage and family more. Pam was excited to have Bill in full-time ministry partnership. She had a long list of tasks that Bill's talent and skill set could complete with excellence. But to Pam, Bill was not enthusiastically embracing the to-do list.

One day, she headed to the gym to do a weight workout. On the way there, she prayed, "God convict Bill. Light a fire under him!"

As was her habit, she listened to the Bible as she exercised. While she was praying about her marriage situation, pumping iron, this verse played in her earbuds: "Therefore I, the prisoner of the Lord, implore you to walk in a manner worthy of the calling with which you have been called, with all humility and gentleness, with patience, showing tolerance for one another in love, being diligent to preserve the unity of the Spirit in the bond of peace (Eph 4:1–3, NASB1995).

God's Spirit seemed to whisper to Pam's heart, *Pam, you are a relationship coach. Are you walking worthy of your calling? How humble have you been lately? Have you been gentle, or have you been pushing your agenda? This is a significant transition*

> **Today's Peace Step**
> In prayer, surrender a slow growth area of a relationship to God, His way, and His timing.

for your husband. How patient have you been? Is there something you can do to preserve unity?

Pam drove straight home and apologized: "Honey, I am sorry I have been demanding. I trust you will move on our ministry task list, in your timing and as God leads."

A few days later, in a quiet time in the Word, God motivated Bill to take swift action without Pam's nagging!

David Low Dodge Passed on His Heart for Peace (Historic Story)

Jesus said, "My kingdom is not of this world. If it were, my servants would fight to prevent my arrest by the Jewish leaders. But now my kingdom is from another place." JOHN 18:36 (NIV)

The thought that he almost killed his landlord led David to question violence and become a peacemaker. The landlord blundered into his room one night by mistake and startled David awake. Due to traveling with large amounts of money, he kept pistols with him and reached for one, but paused in time. Once he chose to pursue peace, he gave up guns.

He became a teacher and started a few schools, including one for girls. His schools became famous due to new educational methods he introduced. David left teaching for business in dry goods, built a large cotton mill in Connecticut, and became a pioneer in the mill industry. His son William, who followed in his faith, became a great businessman whose generosity earned him the title "Christian

Merchant." After the Civil War, William worked on conciliation and harmony among all sectors.

David also spent two years wrestling with his thoughts on peace and war. He knew Jesus did not call for His servants to fight. As a theologian, David believed Christians should not fight and, in 1809, wrote a pamphlet, *The Mediator's Kingdom Not of this World*. Later he published a second pamphlet to share his thoughts on the futility of war.

> **Today's Peace Step**
> Invest time in acts of compassion and kindness to be a peacemaker.

David gathered with about thirty friends in 1815 and formed the New York Peace Society, four months before Noah Worcester formed a similar group in Boston. David's society worked for many years, and in 1928 their society joined with other peace groups to form the American Peace Society.

David and his son William believed war hardened hearts and chose to follow Christ in love, kindness, and compassion, and built a legacy of peace and faith.

Peace Through Conflict Resolution by PeggySue Wells

"If possible, so far as it depends on you, live peaceably with all." ROMANS 12:18 (ESV)

One morning, Mom tried to cheer her grumpy teen with tea and pancakes. When her teen remained sullen, Mom felt tempted to dish back negativity with the silent treatment followed by a barbed jab.

She could easily say, "Is your homework done? You know you better keep those grades above C level."

If we're doing our best to live peaceably, why does conflict continue to escalate between those we love, neighbors, community members, political parties, and world governments? As families, coworkers, and fellow inhabitants of planet Earth, we have gotten really good at being in the five downward-spiraling relational Rs. The process goes like this:

1. Something happens or is said, done, not said, or not done that results in someone feeling **rejected**.
2. Rejection is a lousy feeling, so we become **resentful** about feeling rejected. We make up a story about why the individual acts this way.
3. Feeling resentment, we **resist** relationship with the silent treatment.
4. Resistance leads to **revenge** and wanting another to feel hurt.
5. **Repeat.** Unresolved, this cycle repeats until a relationship is damaged beyond repair.

These are the five Rs that spell destruction to relationships: rejection, resentment, resistance, revenge, repeat.

The life-giving, life-changing solution comes by sticking to the facts and letting the facts stand for themselves.

To her grousing teen, Mom said, "The story I'm making up in my head is that you'd rather be anywhere than with me."

Her teen responded with a completely baffled expression. "I just learned the boy I babysit has leukemia."

Most things people say or do, don't say, don't do, and accidentally do or don't do hardly ever have anything to do with us. We're living our lives as well as we can. And the best we can do has everything to do with sticking to the facts and not making up stories in our head.

> **Today's Peace Step**
> Use PeggySue's life-giving solution when you find resentment building up.

Week 19

Peaceful Debates

Prayer for Peaceful Discussions

Dear Lord, Paul debated with many people to spread the gospel of peace and love. He reasoned rather than argued. He made disciples this way, encouraging people to discover truth and follow Christ. Help me share your way with reason and careful debate. Lord Jesus, you also debated and responded to attacks by calmly asking questions or sharing a parable. Give me wisdom to follow your example.

Let me be an instrument of peace and realize that can come with words accompanied by compassion and love. Let my actions speak for me, too, as ways to open hearts for sharing thoughts and exchanging ideas. Provide opportunities and time to speak up and help others understand your sacrifice and gift of eternal life.

Wisdom from Young Peacemakers

I try not to get mad.

Make peace by making people be calm.

Life Debate

But in your hearts revere Christ as Lord. Always be prepared to give an answer to everyone who asks you to give the reason for the hope that you have. But do this with gentleness and respect. 1 PETER *3:15 (NIV)*

As part of her English class in high school Karen had to debate. The topic was life and birth control, way before abortion came to the forefront. She served on the con side. In researching the topic Karen looked at what arguments the other side might bring up. The birth control methods were new but not its morality, although not directly covered in the morality in the Bible.

Prepared for the topic, Karen responded to the possible arguments from Genesis 38:8–11 when Onan practiced an early form of birth control and God killed him for it. She went on to share the domino effect and that not valuing life begins when people move from viewing children as a blessing and inheritance from God (Psalm 127:3) to an inconvenience. That could lead to acceptance of abortion. Her team won the debate, but most people forgot the reasoning involved.

> **Today's Peace Step**
> Applaud pregnant women and affirm older people to fill their hearts with hope.

Over the years Karen watched what she outlined could happen in the future unfold. She saw people move further over the cliff to justify taking lives and not valuing children or the aged. Most disheartening was the unseen: as people value life less, suicide rates skyrocket. This results from lack of strong relationships when people put goals, careers, and personal desires above loved ones. Karen recalls the antidote in the debate of trusting all life to God.

Love and hope counter all the deaths and unwanted feelings of people. Karen married and had five children she treasures, and they are now raising families and still close to one another. She and her family affirm one another, celebrate life, and remind others they matter.

Bereans Reason with Paul (Biblical Story)

Now these people were more noble-minded than those in Thessalonica, for they received the word with great eagerness, examining the Scriptures daily to see whether these things were so. ACTS 17:11

Paul was often chased away from the cities where he preached. Sometimes that involved stonings and beatings. He never knew what to expect as he entered a new place. He left Thessalonica after the Jews stirred up a mob and caused an uproar. The mob shouted that these men had upset the world.

Next, Paul entered Berea along with his companion, Silas. What a delight for Paul to find men eager to examine the Scriptures and debate with enthusiasm. The news reached the people of Thessalonica, and they came after Paul and stirred up crowds. Friends escorted Paul to Athens. Later, Paul spent time in Macedonia, and Sopater from Berea accompanied him. Sopater reflected the lasting change of a convert.

God struck Paul with a bolt of lightning, but Paul never asked God to strike any of his accusers or abusers. He had turned his back on violence and his work as a troublemaker when he became a follower of Christ. Paul understood the anger of men who sought to destroy him, for he had been out to destroy the followers of Christ in his past (Acts 9:1), who had described Paul as breathing threats and murder. After encountering Christ, Paul stated in Romans 12:18, "If possible, so far as it depends on you, be at peace with all people." He boldly walked into each city ready to proclaim Christ, knowing he might die for his faith. His courage came from God. Paul greeted people with words of grace and peace. He urged others to live in peace (1 Thessalonians 5:13). He replaced his sword and horse with words of peace and sandals.

> **Today's Peace Step**
> Lean on God for inner peace and strength to be calm.

Leadership with Reason

"Blessed are the peacemakers, for they will be called sons of God." MATTHEW 5:9

Jim fielded lots of calls. It seemed all three ministry leaders for youth were upset with one another. He listed all the complaints and prayed over the list. He entered the classroom for the Monday leaders' meeting early, wrote the complaints in one column on a chalkboard, and covered it up.

When everyone assembled he opened with a prayer and said, "I've had lots of complaints over the past week, so right now I want each of you to name one positive thing about the ministry and other leaders." It took a bit of prodding, but someone finally opened up with, "I'm happy you're in charge because you are always fair and calm."

The list grew with the positive aspects of fellowship, loving the children they served, that people prayed for each other, and more. Then he showed the complaint list and said, "There are some legitimate complaints that we can address. What we need are possible solutions. For example, it is hard to go to the supply cabinet and find the supply you need that day is out and not on the list of needs. We can do better in writing a note when we take the last of something. Leave a note of where the supply is that day, and maybe only take what you need. Even better, check out a week ahead what you'll need, and note if that supply is low. You could donate the supply or email Tina, who restocks what we need."

> **Today's Peace Step**
> When there's conflict, let people give ideas of possible solutions.

They went through each item, came up with possible solutions, and voted on what to try. By the end of the meeting people laughed and chatted, and members also asked forgiveness if they hoarded supplies or hurt someone's feelings. As people left they thanked Jim and said they appreciated that he had listened and used wise conflict resolution methods.

John Adams (Historic Story)

Your word is a lamp to my feet and a light to my path. PSALM *119:105*

For President John Adams, his strength also became his weakness. He strove for peace, waiting as long as possible to try to negotiate peace with a revolution in the colonies, until he knew the necessity for the war. He worked on many of the founding documents of the United States, but in his heart he desired a greater peace.

Adams wrote to a Zionist friend, "For I really wish the Jews again in Judea an independent nation." He grew up as a Puritan, who considered themselves to be like the Israelites fleeing Egypt. He considered the nation of Israel the most glorious nation that ever lived on earth and stated, "They have given religion to three quarters of the globe and have influenced the affairs of mankind more, and more happily, than any other nation, ancient or modern." His ideas helped begin the Jewish Restoration movement.

> **Today's Peace Step**
> Develop strong relationships in which you build up one another.

John Adams is more known for his diplomacy to negotiate peace with the British and to prevent war between the colonies and France. Peace making kept him away from home and his beloved wife for six years, with only three months together during those years. He took his sons John Quincy and Charles with him at times.

The peace lover in him extended to his family. He and Abigail wrote more than one thousand letters to each other that reveal their great love and enduring friendship. He even addressed her as Miss Adorable in a letter while courting her, although most letters address each other as "my dearest friend." They had both longed for a true soulmate and found that in one another. The unity they had most likely fostered John's desire for peace. He sought and leaned on her advice in their correspondence. He knew their peace in marriage could reflect peace in the world.

To Confront or Not

But if he does not listen to you, take one or two more with you, so that on the testimony of two or three witnesses every matter may be confirmed. MATTHEW *18:16*

Two elders in the church decided to confront their pastor about statements he made contrary to Scripture. They even wrote a letter. Before going they decided to pray again. Both felt convicted that God did not want them to go. As they prayed they were impressed that God was the authority over the preacher, not them. They chose instead to meet weekly to pray for the minister. After several months the minister stood before the congregation and apologized.

He said, "I have been teaching in error, and God has impressed upon me that I need to get the truth right in writing my sermons. I welcome others to help me apply the Word correctly." The two men joined rejoiced and joined in with humble hearts that God led them all in the right path. They had great fellowship wrestling over the Bible weekly.

That story so impressed Marie that she followed the idea. When they moved to a new duty station and she wanted to change churches, her husband said, "No. I don't have time to church hop. We prayed, and God led us here." Marie decided to pray for the pastor. She prayed for two years. On their last Sunday before moving to a new duty station, the pastor read his chosen passage and preached the Word of God. He also explained that in the past week it was like scales fell off his eyes and the Word became alive. He touched Marie's heart.

> **Today's Peace Step**
>
> Let prayer always be your first step before confronting someone.

She prayed, "Lord, why can't I be here longer to hear him now that his eyes and heart are opened?"

She heard a small voice say, "I answered your prayer. You are done praying for him." She remembered that everywhere they moved, and she always prayed for the pastor and church staff.

Week 20

Peace with the Past

Prayer for Past Problems and Moving Forward

Dear Lord, I can relive past struggles of broken relationships, disasters, and abuse. Help me forgive and move forward in life. You have forgiven me, but sometimes I hold on to hurts. Help me let go and be free to face the present and future with hope and joy.

Help me comfort friends as they deal with divorce, loss, and the pain of abuse. You were beaten and crucified, so you understand torture, abuse, and loss of dignity. Be with those who suffer at the hands of wicked people. Give them inner peace that passes understanding. Help them rejoice in you.

Help me move forward with joy as I trust my days to you.

Wisdom from Young Peacemakers

If someone is sad, help them. Grandma was sad when Grandpa died and didn't want to decorate or have parties, so I helped her decorate for Christmas.

I have to really forgive, no matter what. I just deal with it, and I try not to think about it again. It's not fun.

Peace After Divorce by Amy Harden

*"The man who hates and divorces his wife," says the L*ORD*, the God of Israel, "does violence to the one he should protect," says the L*ORD *Almighty. So be on your guard, and do not be unfaithful. M*ALACHI *2:16 (NIV)*

Seeking peace after divorce is a challenging journey if you believe the myth that God forbids all divorce or that all divorce is a sin except for adultery. Malachi 2:16 states that God "hates divorce," but new translations, like the NIV, say, "The man who hates and divorces his wife . . . does violence to the one he should protect."

Not all marriages end due to adulterous actions or the husband hating his wife; many end when the protection that God commands is removed or never felt. The covenant of protection is broken with abuse, neglect, and abandonment. Women in today's culture no longer wait for their husbands to divorce them; they seek protection and peace for themselves.

Amelia believed when married couples are in trouble they should do all they can to save their marriage. Her parents rarely fought and were partners in everything with unconditional love for each other. Amelia's father was an Ephesians husband who protected his wife like the church, while her mother submitted to everything.

Amelia's first husband, Erik, was not a Christian and was an alcoholic who was physically and verbally abusive. She knew his tendencies before marriage but thought he would change after taking their vows. Amelia protected Erik when he went on a binge, violently abused her, and

GROWING A PEACEFUL HEART

devalued her in front of friends. She covered up his abuse for three years until he almost choked her to death one night. A phone call from his mother stopped him.

Her military orders to paradise separated her and her husband. Six months after her transfer, she told Erik she wanted to divorce. Even after a last-ditch effort to save the marriage, God

> **Today's Peace Step**
> Trust God to protect you if that promised protection in marriage is removed.

revealed that Erik would never change. A peace fell over Amelia's spirit as she realized the protection promised had long been removed when Erik first hit her. God was her protector—her peace came from Him.

Abraham and Lot: Broken Relationships (Biblical Story)

No Ammonite or Moabite may enter the assembly of the LORD; none of their descendants, even to the tenth generation, may ever enter the assembly of the LORD. DEUTERONOMY 23:3

Lot's daughters, after the destruction of Sodom and Gomorrah, committed incest with their father. The women gave birth to the nations of the Moabites and Ammonites. Before the nations began Lot and his uncle Abraham had been very close and dwelt together. Problems began when their possession became too many, in Genesis 13. Abraham, a man of peace, suggested they separate and let Lot choose the land he wanted. Lot chose the lush area of Jordan.

When Lot ran into trouble, Abraham bailed him out. That happened when a servant informed Abraham that enemies kidnapped Lot, his family, and all his possessions. Abraham fought and restored Lot, his people, and his possessions. Lot ended up in Sodom and fled with the help of angels before God destroyed the city. However, Lot's daughters lacked trust in God and planned their own way to extend the family that started the Moabites and Ammonites. We don't see the two men talking after that event. It appears they stopped communicating, which left their relationship broken. Read about them in Genesis 13–14.

Generations later, as the Israelites left Egypt and traveled to the Promised Land, the Moabites and Ammonites refused to be hospitable to the Israelites. God then established a rule about the Israelites not marrying either tribe for ten generations. Brokenness can impact many people. It began with hoarding, with accumulating too much stuff. Wealth can be divisive.

> **Today's Peace Step**
> Stay close to God, avoid letting stuff get in the way of family, and communicate with family.

Once the men separated, Lot made poor choices that pulled him away from God. God blessed Abraham more and renewed his promise to make him a great nation. Abraham stayed focused on God's plans. Sometimes choices also involve God's guidance and plan, but alas the broken relationships continue.

Overcoming Grief in Divorce by Joan Benson

Peace I leave you, My peace I give you. . . . Do not let your hearts be troubled, nor fearful. JOHN 14:27

She sat fixated on the door David had shut moments before. Joan's once-captive tears erupted into a hurricane of pain. They had dated for six years and were married for twenty-two. He had been her best friend from age fifteen. How could he leave?

"Why, God? How could he love another woman?" He retired from his airline career to go into ministry ten years prior. Pounding the kitchen counter with her fist, she screamed, "No, no, no! This can't be." Joan's world of family, church, and friends was shattered like broken glass with one final closed door.

One day driving to work, Joan noticed a runner on the beach. *I might try running to help me sleep*, she thought. Joan was not a runner—she had never been one. Converting emotional pain through physical pain was easy to accomplish. As Christian music played on her small recorder, words of faith poured like healing oil over her numb heart. As she pounded the pavement, God's presence became tangible. She was not alone. Like the starlight in the summer sky, God's light invaded her dark soul night after night.

Surprises of "God-hugs" strengthened her. Kind words, a hug from a colleague, neighbor, or youngster she barely knew felt like God's love reaching down from heaven.

One time she drove to the beach for solace. Instead of peace, she was knocked about in a swirl of wild waves. In her spirit, she heard, "Look out, not down." When she did, she noticed a beautiful design on the beach as far as she could see. God wanted to turn Joan's mess into beauty *if she trusted Him.*

Over time, Joan discovered peace as she let go. Releasing the one who hurt her so while trusting God as her source of hope brought peace and purpose.

> **Today's Peace Step**
> Take time to talk to God, rest, and leave worries in His care.

Corrie ten Boom and Forgiveness (Historic Story)

Hatred stirs up strife, but love covers all offenses. PROVERBS 10:12

"When we confess our sins, God casts them into the deepest ocean, gone forever," Corrie ten Boom said in 1947 in a church in Munich. She thought she understood forgiveness. Afterall, she had studied the Bible and followed Jesus all her life, but the next moments tested her.

Corrie froze as the heavyset camp guard responsible for her sister Betsie's death made his way to her and held out his hand and asked for forgiveness. He said, "I became a Christian after the war. Your message about forgiveness touched me very much. You told about camp Ravensbrück. I was a camp guard there. I have always wanted to ask forgiveness of someone personally, so I ask you: Will you forgive me?" She paused, unable to take his hand, and prayed. He wore an overcoat and brown hat. Memories flooded her mind of her poor thin sister, naked, walking past the man who had a leather crop swinging from his belt.

GROWING A PEACEFUL HEART

At that moment Corrie realized that forgiveness is an act of will, not an emotion, and she grasped his hand. As soon as Corrie held his hand she felt a warm wave pass through her body to her hand. She cried out, "I forgive you, brother, with all my heart." She said that's when she experienced God's love the most deeply.

Corrie declared it was not easy to forgive and let go of pain. She converted her home to house victims of Nazi brutality, where she ministered to them and encouraged them to forgive. Corrie wrestled with forgiveness at various times, including a time when friends wounded her. She had to let go to find true freedom that forgiveness brings. She also helped transform a former concentration camp into a refugee center, where flower boxes added to every window brought beauty.

> **Today's Peace Step**
> Forgive even when
> you don't feel
> you can do it.

Peace Amid Holidays by PeggySue Wells

Surely you have granted him unending blessings and made him glad with the joy of your presence. PSALM 21:6 (NIV)

"I hate the holidays," her daughter groused, reluctant to set up Christmas decorations.

Her sister nodded. "I hate birthdays."

Mom's heart sank. Of course, she wanted family celebrations to be Hallmark memorable. They were memorable, all right, but not Hallmark style, no matter how hard she tried.

Her daughter voiced what her mother had often thought. "Can we just go away for the holidays? Come back when it's over?"

Can we avoid the disappointment of unmet hopes that this time, this year, that the words and actions of those we love most would not pierce? Sidestep comparisons, barbed comments, and circles drawn that leave vulnerable family members excluded.

"The holidays are when the offices of family law attorneys receive the most calls," a lawyer shared. "Someone doesn't keep to the visitation agreement or changes arrangements that crush carefully planned celebrations. There are a lot of moving parts, a lot of emotions, and a lot of hopes, traditions, and expectations balanced on these landmark days."

Reeling from emotional blows can affect us emotionally, financially, physically, and spiritually and rob us of joy. Yet it's a precious season with the Lord to grow, learn, rest, and yield. God of the universe is actively at work in us, our children, and the lives and hearts of those who hurt us.

Make holidays easier. Schedule periods away from the phone, household responsibilities, and the noise of the electronics to journal, pray, read, walk, and listen. Mostly listen.

Take mini vacations. Exercise, watch a comedy, attend the church worship service, take a walk, and read a good book. Have tea with a friend and allow only eight minutes to talk about the negative. Then shift the conversation to options, potential, possibilities, and solutions. Help children refresh. Play a game, read books at the library, visit the park, or volunteer in the community, and include unstructured time.

Holidays and relationships may not always measure up to expectations, so build in de-stressors.

> **Today's Peace Step**
> List activities that relax you, and include them in holiday plans.

Week 21

Peace with Money

Prayer for Finances and Contentment with Money

Dear Lord, I want to focus on you, but there are bills to pay and mouths to feed. It seems there's no end of ways to spend money and so little left to save. Help our family not worry about money but to trust you to provide what we need. Help us to not desire more than we are able to buy. Let us be content with the blessings you give us.

When I am blessed with money, let me not be greedy and spend it on my desires. Help me be generous.

Let us seek you and your will and trust that you will care for our needs. Help us not fight over money or use it as a weapon or tool to manipulate each other. Bless us with wisdom to know how to budget our money and the strength to stay within the budget. Help us use our blessings to bless others and share what you give us. Let us have generous hearts and hands.

Wisdom from Young Peacemakers

Money makes people argue. I think we need to get rid of money.

If God gave everyone enough money, like $10, we wouldn't fight.

A Bumpy Financial Start

Make sure that your character is free from the love of money, being content with what you have; for He Himself has said, "I will never desert you, nor will I ever abandon you." HEBREWS 13:5

Patsy overflowed with joy at the quick ceremony of marriage the day before her new husband left for a two-month deployment at sea. She dressed up, and he wore his uniform. His commanding officer and the captain of the ship and their families witnessed the ceremony. The captain took everyone out to dinner afterward.

However, her husband forgot to set up for her to receive any pay or to give her the phone numbers of any of the wives. She had a job, so he thought she'd be fine.

Alas, Patsy lost her job and didn't know what to do. She sold almost all their possessions to pay the bills. The ship's mail was also lost during the middle of the deployment, and she felt hurt and angry that her new husband never sent mail. He came home shocked to find only a bed in the apartment. He quickly changed his pay and bank accounts to include her, helped her find a new job, and above all, apologized.

Today's Peace Step

In marriage always be sure to discuss money, share finances, and have emergency plans.

Patsy also started attending events with the ship's families and made connections to be in touch the next time the ship deployed. He also invited his parents to visit so they could get acquainted, and they told her to call on them when she had any future problems.

It's not easy to have such a rough start in a marriage and to be so disconnected. Patsy and her husband made it past the difficult start because they forgave each another, both had a good sense of humor, and they developed a good support system. They were more in love with each other than money and things.

Peter and Contentment (Biblical Story)

You younger men, likewise, be subject to your elders; and all of you, clothe yourselves with humility toward one another, because God is opposed to the proud, but He gives grace to the humble. 1 PETER 5:5

Peter responded to the encouragement of Jesus to let down their nets with willingness even though they had caught nothing all night. The nets filled and had too many fish to bring in, so they called for help. The miracle caused Peter to confess his unworthiness, and he left everything to follow Jesus. That did not make Peter perfect.

Impulsive Peter often raced in without thinking, such as trying to rebuke Jesus when He stated that He would be killed (Mark 8:33). Jesus rebuked Peter. He told tax collectors that Jesus paid tax. Jesus used a coin in a fish's mouth to provide the money but scolded Peter. Peter also denied he knew Jesus three times as Jesus had predicted (Matthew 26:69–74). And at the picnic on the beach, when

Jesus questioned Peter's love, Peter asked Jesus about John. Jesus turned Peter's focus back to Himself when He said, "You follow Me!" (John 21:22)

Jesus patiently worked with Peter, who also loved Jesus greatly. After being filled with the Holy Spirit, Peter became a bold leader, bringing 3000 people to believe in Jesus in one talk. That inspired the daily teachings and breaking bread together. Peter and the other disciples realized the calling meant discipling other believers. That mattered more than wealth.

> **Today's Peace Step**
> Think of God and others before yourself.

Peter shared that we must be clothed with humility and avoid greed (1 Peter 5:2). Greed keeps people from being content, while humility, the absence of pride, keeps our focus off ourselves and expectation that we deserve anything. That's part of the secret to contentment. We can be like Peter if we put God first and learn to be happy with God's blessings for us.

Tithing When Bills are Due

"For this reason I say to you, do not be worried about your life, as to what you will eat or what you will drink; nor for your body, as to what you will put on. Is life not more than food, and the body more than clothing?" MATTHEW 6:25

Darlene and her husband faced years of financial problems. It culminated in bankruptcy. That eased their stresses because it consolidated bills due and dropped others. Her husband graduated top of his class, but was never able to get a medical residency, and the bills for medical school plus the inability to get a good-paying job made finances difficult. Family helped, and they both worked whatever they could find while raising their children. The one thing they worked on was to give to God both money and time. She learned not to count pennies or worry but to trust God.

In spite of earning less than the bills totaled they found the money to pay the bills and feed the family. Then her husband returned to school to become a nurse in a one-year program for others like him with a medical background. Darlene signed up to be a shopper for groceries and take-out foods. She worked hard to meet a set weekly goal that would cover the bills. Then the pandemic hit, and God blessed her work. Her job, deemed essential, meant she could work. Her clients needed her more than ever, and she quickly doubled her income.

They saved all they could for a year, and then her husband graduated and could only get a job in another state. They had the savings to move. Once her husband started his job she found she could not make nearly as much in the new area and could only work two days a week. Her little bit was just

> **Today's Peace Step**
> Be generous to God, trust instead of worrying, and He will supply your needs.

enough to cover the rest of their expenses and unexpected bills. Her husband soon received a raise and started working overtime twice a month. They continue to tithe and trust God will continue to care for their needs.

Eisenhower: In God We Trust (Historic Story)

There is one body and one Spirit, just as you also were called in one hope of your calling. EPHESIANS *4:4*

Pastor David and his wife, Ida, raised their seven sons in the River Brethren Church, an offshoot of the Mennonite faith. The denomination did not believe in child baptism, and ten days after being sworn in as president of the Untied States, Ike Eisenhower asked to be baptized at the National Presbyterian Church in a private ceremony.

Ike began his inaugural address with a short prayer he wrote, initiated the National Prayer Breakfast, and began his cabinet meetings with prayer. He approved the decision of Congress to add "under God" to the Pledge of Allegiance and made "In God We Trust" the country's official motto. Eisenhower believed that religious faith and freedom were the most important difference from communism. He oversaw D-Day and the landing of soldiers in Normandy that led to Germany's surrender and the end of World War II. He also ended the Korean War.

> **Today's Peace Step**
> Dwell on Scriptures, and be thankful for freedom to worship.

On February 7, 1954, in a radio address, Eisenhower gave a civics lesson about the connection between pilgrims, George Washington, and Abraham Lincoln that lay in their shared steadfast belief in God. He said, "By the millions, we speak prayers, we sing hymns, and no matter what their words may be, their spirit is the same: *In God is our Trust.*"

Eisenhower served in the army and rose to the rank of general, defeating countries who wanted to suppress religious freedom. He encouraged Americans to dwell on the virtues of courage, self-confidence, and an unshakable belief in the Bible. He believed the success of the country rested on faith and enterprise. He believed in peace and said, "Every gun that is made, every warship launched, every rocket fired signifies, in the final sense, a theft from those who hunger and are not fed, those who are cold and are not clothed."

Job Loss

And my God will supply all your needs according to His riches in glory in Christ Jesus. PHILIPPIANS 4:19

Jim retired from the military ready to start a new career. The next day Jim received news that the man who planned to hire Jim and make him his partner and business heir had crashed in the Everglades and died. No job! He started seeking a new job and after a few months got one with a cruise line. They fired him after a few months because they said they no longer needed him. That really hurt until he read that they had gone bankrupt, and he realized they slowly let everyone go. He and his wife trusted that the unexpected losses meant God had something better planned. They trusted it would all work out in God's time and felt peace.

Jim spent months working part time for a friend, cleaning carpets for other friends and stretching the retirement money while their oldest child began college. He also attended an organization that helped people find jobs, and he worked on his résumé. He found a slightly better job with a refrigeration company. At last, he got an engineering job in the space industry, but it was four hours from home. He stayed with his mom for a while and then rented an apartment as they waited for a few of the middle children to graduate from high school. His wife began writing at that time, but in her first year she only earned one dollar a day. They believed God called her to write instead of returning to her past computer career. She found a magazine that paid quickly to meet unexpected bills. She became well published, but it took time.

Today's Peace Step
Trust God while persisting to overcome financial challenges.

Then, someone he networked with at church helped him land a job in his field as a naval architect. That became the career that lasted the rest of his life. The experiences gave him more compassion for his children and friends when they faced financial difficulties. He could share how God provided for his family when he lacked the income needed.

Week 22

Peace and Compassion with Grace

Prayer for a Christ-Like Heart

Father in heaven, you have said that we are to love the Lord our God with all our heart and with all our soul and with all our mind. May your love produce compassion and grace in my heart. I am grateful that you sent people to comfort me when I felt pain and hurt. May those memories help me understand the hurt and pain others experience and help me be compassionate.

Help me to always think of others first and understand them. Let me seek to ease suffering and hurt in the people around me. Help me be more caring and to reach out with kindness. Let my actions lift the spirits of others and help them have peace in the midst of troubles and heartaches.

Wisdom from Young Peacemakers

I have peace with my brother and sister when I stop and do something that makes them happy.

When someone has an owie it hurts. I want to hug them and make them smile.

Brotherly Love

Love each other as I have loved you. Greater love has no one than this: to lay down one's life for one's friends. JOHN 15:12–13 (NIV)

Johnny was surprised to hear that his sister Mary now had the same illness he had recovered from two years earlier. The news broke his heart because he had always loved his sister and hated to see her endure what he had been through. He also thought back to the time of his illness and how difficult it had been for his parents. How must they feel now with Mary in the same plight?

Johnny soon learned that the only way to save Mary would be a blood transfusion from someone who had previously conquered the disease. Since the siblings had the same rare blood type, Johnny was an ideal candidate.

The doctor asked, "Would you be willing to give your blood to Mary?"

Johnny hesitated. He began to tremble, and his eyes revealed deep thought. Soon, however, he smiled back to the doctor and said, "She is my sister. Yes, I will!"

> **Today's Peace Step**
> Evaluate how much you are willing to sacrifice for those you love.

Soon medical personnel wheeled the children into a hospital room. Johnny looked healthy, but Mary looked pale and thin. When their eyes met, Johnny gave Mary a big smile as if to say, "We can do it."

It didn't take long for the nurse to insert a needle in Johnny's arm. As he watched his blood flow through the tube Johnny's smile faded and, with the transfusion almost over, Johnny turned to the doctor and asked, "When will I die?"

Now the doctor and nurse realized why Johnny had hesitated. They understood his frightened look and trembling voice. Johnny had believed that giving his blood to his sister would mean giving up his life, yet he chose to do it: a profound decision and example of unlimited love!

Compassion in Dire Straits (Historic Story)

Praise be to the God and Father of our Lord Jesus Christ, the Father of compassion and the God of all comfort, who comforts us in all our troubles, so that we can comfort those in any trouble with the comfort we ourselves have received from God. 2 CORINTHIANS 1:3–4 (NIV)

One cold winter night during the Civil War a regiment of Confederate soldiers camped on the ground. It began to snow. A number of them probably wondered if they would be killed by another enemy: the weather. The snow continued all through the night.

As morning finally approached, their commander suddenly realized he felt comfortable, even warm. What had happened? His eyes fell on the warm blanket draped over his body and then he saw him. Yes, it was a young private rubbing his hands together and stomping the ground to stay alive. This young soldier had forfeited his own cover and given it to his superior. Compassion comes in many colors.

A second story from the same war adds another dimension. This time Union soldiers were closing in on their enemy. One Confederate soldier was severely wounded and thought, *Okay, this is it! They will kill me!*

Then, to his surprise, he saw a young black face look at him. Without hesitation, this Union soldier picked him up and carefully carried him to a safe and secluded place. At this point the wounded soldier recognized his rescuer. For a moment they simply looked at one another and smiled, as both recalled the days they played together in childhood. Friendship bridges differences. Compassion comes in many colors, and God works in mysterious ways!

> **Today's Peace Step**
> Show compassion to others, even when your life is hard, or you have different world views.

The Helping Hand

Therefore, encourage one another and build one another up, just as you also are doing. 1 THESSALONIANS 5:11

Mark walked home from school one day when he saw another young man in front of him trip and fall to the ground. The guy's books, sweater, baseball, and other items flew out of his arms and scattered everywhere, so Mark hurried to help. The boys chatted as they continued their walk, and Mark felt he had a new friend when they reached Bill's house. He invited him in for a Coke and a chat. The baseball and other objects opened up items to discuss and revealed common interests.

Over the next few months and years, the boys visited occasionally. Finally, when high school graduation was only weeks away, Bill asked Mark if they might have a chat. It didn't take long for Bill to explain why he had made the request.

"Mark, I know you probably remember how we first met."

Mark nodded and waited for Bill to continue.

"Well, when you helped me that day you probably wondered why I had so much stuff. You see, I had just cleaned out my locker because I was going home to kill myself."

"What? You don't mean that, do you?"

"Yes, I had been saving some of my mother's pills, and I had enough to do the job. Somehow, after your help and kindness I realized I didn't want to die. You did more than pick up my stuff. You saved my life!"

One little act of kindness seems like a trivial action, but it can be life changing to the receiver. Each day, ask God to put someone in your path whom you can bless with a compassionate word or deed. Let God use you to change hearts and bring inner peace to someone who is troubled.

> **Today's Peace Step**
> Show compassion and concern today. You never know what your words might mean to someone.

Dreams and Reality (Biblical Story)

Pharaoh said to Joseph, "I have had a dream, but no one can interpret it; and I have heard it said about you, that when you hear a dream you can interpret it." GENESIS 41:15

In the Old Testament Joseph lived with many ups and downs. Jacob gave him, his favorite son, a magnificent coat. God also favored him and gave him dreams about his siblings bowing down to him. Naturally, sharing the dreams made his eleven brothers jealous—so jealous, in fact, that ten of them plotted to kill him. One brother named Reuben suggested they put Joseph in a well instead so he could slip back later to retrieve him.

Reuben's plan didn't materialize because a caravan of Egyptians passed by, and brother Judah suggested they sell Joseph to them. God blessed Joseph wherever he landed. Even in prison, the guards put him in charge of the prisoners. He interpreted dreams for two imprisoned men who served Pharaoh. God used dreams to bring change for Joseph.

He interpreted Pharaoh's dream concerning a future famine. Pharaoh placed Joseph in charge of all the land of Egypt, where he wisely stored grain in separate silos around the land. Keeping it separate prevented any disease from spreading in the grain. Eventually, Joseph offered food to his brothers who sold him and shared that with what they meant to do to harm him, God used for good that helped them all. He had compassion and held nothing against his brothers. Read Joseph's story in Genesis 37–50 to discover a clear picture of compassion.

Today's Peace Step

Whatever problem you are facing, remember you are never out of God's sight or security.

Of course, the most beautiful picture of compassion and grace is found in Christ; all of Scripture points ultimately to him. Acts 10:38 tells us he went about "doing good." Christ healed the sick, lame, deaf, mute, and lepers. He even brought the dead back to life. His compassion and love bring us peace when we also trust that God uses everything for our good.

An Uncle's Understanding (Historic Story)

For the moment, all discipline seems not to be pleasant, but painful; yet to those who have been trained by it, afterward it yields the peaceful fruit of righteousness. HEBREWS *12:11*

When Sara's husband's uncle passed away a number of years ago, they attended his service in Huntsville, Alabama. Uncle Foyl had been a prominent educator for over fifty years, serving as both an elementary teacher and principal.

Sara smiled and watched Bill nod in agreement during the memorial service as the pastor enumerated some of his uncle's accomplishments. However, what she remembered most happened later at the gravesite.

It was mid-afternoon and Bill started to say goodbye to a few folks when Sara saw a man who appeared as though he didn't want to leave. Feeling a bit awkward when he glanced up at her, she asked, "Was Foyl a special friend of yours?"

"Oh, yes," he responded. "Mr. DuBose was like a parent to me!"

"Really? How was that?"

"Well, many years ago I was a hoodlum of the worst sort, and Mr. DuBose called me to the principal's office for correction. Now folks don't think much of spanking, but DuBose gave me what I needed: an old-fashion whipping. Then he gave me a job. He sent me around the whole school to scrape and clean windows and attend to whatever needed attention. Through it all—the spanking and the work assignment—I saw his concern and compassion. He changed my life through his love. I became a new man."

Today's Peace Step

If you have a child, grandchild, or other relative who needs your love and discipline, ask God to direct you, and follow through to help shape the child's character.

Taking time to correct and discipline the lad made him realize his principal cared about him. It produced a harvest of peace and showed the boy a new way to live.

Foyl's compassion helped the man let go of anger, feel peace, and change his heart.

Week 23

Getting Along with Others through Personalities

Prayer for Acceptance and Peace
with All Personalities

Dear Lord, you made us all wonderfully unique. Part of your design as you formed us in the womb included shaping our personalities. Help me be content as the person you made me to be and be thankful for the different personalities around me. Give me understanding that I might live at peace with loved ones as well as people I merely encounter.

Help me rejoice at differences and appreciate the strengths of others. Help me overcome my weaknesses and use my strengths to help others. In conflicts, may I consider the goals of each personality involved and what they need. May we learn to appreciate one another and work together in harmony. May we rejoice at our differences and use them to build community.

Wisdom from Young Peacemakers

I smile and talk a lot. My brother doesn't talk much, but he listens, and that's nice. It's good we're different.

We don't have to act the same or like the same things to like each other.

Mother–Daughter Harmony through Understanding

For this reason also, since the day we heard of it, we have not ceased to pray for you and to ask that you may be filled with the knowledge of His will in all spiritual wisdom. COLOSSIANS *1:9 (NASB1995)*

Even as a teen Chris strove for peace. Her college application essay focused on the goal of peace of mind. But years later, life with her youngest child disrupted any peace. Chris thought, *Why can't I get along with my daughter? Macayle is so stubborn and strong willed. Even bedtime every night is a hassle. She is so rebellious.*

When Macayle turned ten, Chris desperately searched for solutions. Finally, she read a book that changed her life, one that explained her daughter's personality. She realized that she had never really understood her little girl. She realized her daughter set goals and tenaciously worked to reach them. Chris chose to change and work with her daughter's personality and respect her decisions. She replaced negative words with positive ones like *tenacious* and *very focused*. She accepted Macayle as the wonderful child God made.

She watched the change in their relationship with wonder and joy. She also used her own personality's strength of humor to nurture their bonds. She gave up trying to read books at bedtime that she liked and offered her daughter time to read books of her choice. She realized her daughter didn't hate reading but had different tastes in what she wanted to read.

Chris also started giving her daughter two choices that were both good choices rather than trying to force one on her. Thus, Chris stopped trying to control and let her daughter make decisions. It might be as simple as cleaning her room that day or choosing the day she would clean in the coming week. Her daughter's goal-driven personality, which wanted control, preferred to be able to make choices and set schedules.

Understanding personalities helped Chris in all her relationships, especially with her mother and husband, who had that same powerful director personality as her daughter.

Jacob and Esau: Twins Different in Every Way (Biblical Story)

"Please accept my gift which has been brought to you [Esau], because God has dealt graciously with me and because I have plenty." So he [Jacob] urged him, and he accepted it. GENESIS 33:11

Jacob, a quiet, gentle child and deep thinker, farmed and stayed near home. His twin, Esau, a rugged, hairy man, loved hunting and trapsing around. Their mom, Rebekah, asked God to explain the struggle in her womb, and God said the older one would serve the younger twin (Genesis 25:21–27). Jacob always wanted what his brother had and never waited for God to handle things. Esau never appreciated his birthright and easily gave it away for a bowl of stew. They both knew their grandfather Abraham, but they did not live their faith like him.

Esau turned away from his people and married unbelieving women. Jacob became a con artist who tricked his father into blessing him instead of his brother. Rebecca did not inquire of God when she encouraged Jacob to deceive his father, Isaac. Abraham fell for the trick and had ignored God's call for Jacob, but in the end he actually blessed Jacob: "Be master of your brother and may your mother's sons bow down to you." Selfishness tore the family apart and separated the twins for years because Jacob fled to avoid his brother's vendetta to kill him (Genesis 27:1–41).

During the years away, Laban, Jacob's father-in-law, conned Jacob, yet God blessed Jacob (Genesis 29; 30:27–43). Jacob finally set out for his homeland with all his family and possessions. The night before meeting Esau Jacob spent time alone wrestling with God. He wanted God to personally bless him, still longing for the real blessing. God did, and Jacob faced his brother humbly, ready to bless him. Esau raced to Jacob to embrace and kiss him. He showed he had changed too. Neither man sought what the other had but had learned to be content

> **Today's Peace Step**
> Realize that God is the only one who can supply your deep needs, and stop trying to satisfy your needs through other people.

GROWING A PEACEFUL HEART

with what God gave them and their uniqueness. When their father died, they buried him together. They lived in peace, although one remained a quiet thinker and the other an outgoing hunter.

Inner Peace Through Personalities by Linda Gilden

I will give thanks to You, because I am awesomely and wonderfully made; Wonderful are your works, and my soul knows it very well. PSALM 139:14

For years MaryJo did not understand why everyone seemed more at peace with who they were than she, more involved with other people than she, and more relaxed in social situations. MaryJo decided she was just socially awkward and did not know how to interact with others. Then she stumbled on the knowledge of the personalities.

MaryJo began to study the personalities and quickly learned that mobilizers, socializers, stabilizers, and organizers view the world differently. MaryJo is an organizer and has tendencies toward perfectionism, which was making her and all those around her miserable. She is also a deep thinker and rarely initiates a conversation unless she has something she really wants to say. Once MaryJo learned more about her personality, she was more comfortable in crowds. The times she went to dinner with those of other personalities and sat silently just listening to the conversation were okay. In fact, they were more than okay. They were freeing. Now that MaryJo understood more about the different personalities, she allowed herself to be who she was without being critical.

God made each person unique. We differ from those around us in many ways. Not only do we look differently, but, like MaryJo, we may act differently because our personalities often dictate our actions and reactions.

> **Today's Peace Step**
> Understanding personalities brings peace and freedom to be who God made you to be.

What about you? Have you embraced your uniqueness? When you find yourself in an uncomfortable situation, can you identify what part of your personality makes you feel that way? Can you recognize that you are perfect the way God made you and embrace the real you?

For MaryJo, along with the peace came the freedom to be herself in every situation without worrying about the reactions of others.

Conrad Weiser

"The second is this: 'You shall love your neighbor as yourself.' There is no other commandment greater than these."
MARK 12:31

The widower Johann Conrad Weiser moved from Germany to Livingston Manor, New York, with his children in 1710. When his son Conrad turned fifteen, Johann sent him to live with neighbors of the Iroquois tribe to learn their language and customs. Conrad hated his eight months there but made some friends and learned the language. After he married, Conrad lived on land adjoining his Iroquois friends. They got along and loved one another. Conrad became a peacemaker with the Iroquois.

In 1729 Conrad moved his family to Pennsylvania, and two years later the governor placed him in charge of all Indian affairs. In 1732 Conrad served as an interpreter at the first official meeting with the Pennsylvania provincial leaders. He met Chief Shikellamy, who had been sent to rule over the Delaware and Shawnee nations. The chief expressed joy at meeting a white man who spoke his language and understood his customs and problems. They developed a strong partnership and became a witness to all transactions between the Six Nations.

Conrad and his wife had fourteen children. His friendship with the Indians helped defeat the French in the French and Indian War, and the Native Americans gave Conrad the name of Tarachiawagon, meaning "holder of the heavens." He negotiated the 1758 Treaty of Easton that ended many of the eastern Pennsylvania Indian raids. Conrad promoted the missions to the Indians that the Moravian church established. He served in his community, including as the first justice of the peace.

> **Today's Peace Step**
> Seek to understand your neighbors and people from different cultures.

When Conrad died, one Iroquois leader said, "We are at a great loss and sit in darkness . . . as since his death we cannot so well understand one another." He convinced the Six Nations to not take part in the French and English quarrels.

Newspaper Clients

It is not this way among you, but whoever wants to become prominent among you shall be your servant. MATTHEW 20:26

Rebecca explained to her parents her opportunity to deliver newspapers. They thought she was young but listened as she said, "I can do this. I already wake up early, and it's just our street and a few other houses. We know our neighbors."

They agreed, but she'd have to stick with it at least six months. A neighbor stopped by and asked if Rebecca would be delivering the paper. It seemed the current situation had him very upset because the delivery person showed up late or not at all some days. After he left, Rebecca's mom explained that he would be a customer who always wanted the paper on time or he would call about delays. He was a businessman who counted on the paper with his breakfast, the same time every day. He liked to be in control. Rebecca put him first on the list because he lived only two houses away. She'd start in that direction.

> **Today's Peace Step**
> Treat people according to their personality needs.

She soon learned that the tough part was collecting the money owed. Some people responded to a bill with the Friday paper and returned the envelope with the payment. Others seemed to get distracted and forgot to pay, while others wanted her to come in person in the evening to collect so they could chat with her and catch up on neighborhood news. It took time for her to understand the different personalities and how to respond to each.

She quickly figured out who appreciated being called when there was any delay in the delivery. Others liked to sleep in and preferred not to get a morning call. She liked her customers and their different personalities. She also enjoyed making things. She created ornaments for her customers at Christmas to express appreciation. She rejoiced that so many people generously tipped her, especially the more socializing and thoughtful ones.

Week 24

Peace with Gentleness and Humility

A Prayer for a Spirit-Filled Life

Lord, may we not live in selfish ambition but in humility, always consider the needs of others. Let us strive for peace and correct others with gentle words. May we reach out to people with a gentle touch and humbly praise them. Let our actions reflect your own humility as you washed the feet of your closest friends, fed the hungry, and responded to needs.

Nurture out hearts so that the right spiritual fruit will grow in us. Then we will be filled with love, joy, peace, patience, kindness, goodness, faithfulness, gentleness, and self-control. May those character traits help us bring peace to our family, community, and world. May we pass on the peace you give us.

Wisdom from Young Peacemakers

Everyone should have a therapy hamster.

I can be gentle even when I get angry. I can hit my sister with my soft stuffed animal.

Where is Your Heart?

Do nothing out of selfish ambition or vain conceit, but in humility value others above yourselves. PHILIPPIANS *2:3 (NIV)*

One day Sue and her daughter visited the zoo and noticed another little girl standing in line with her grandmother. The children waited to have tiger paws painted on their faces by a local artist.

Suddenly, a little boy cried out, "There no place to paint anything on your face. You have too many freckles." Embarrassed, the child lowered her head.

At this point, the child's grandmother dropped to her knees and said, "I love your freckles."

"Well, I don't," the child whimpered.

Tracing her finger across the child's cheek, the grandmother continued, "When I was a little girl I always wanted freckles. Freckles are beautiful!"

The child looked up and asked, "Really?"

"Yes, of course. Why, just name me one thing that's prettier than freckles."

Peering into the old woman's smiling face, the little girl softly replied, "Wrinkles."

Sue Monk Kidd then said that in that moment she heard a whisper filled with godly wisdom: "If I look at others with the eyes of love, I will not see blemishes. Only beauty."

Taking it to a higher level than freckles and wrinkles, we can, and should, pursue every relationship with the eyes of love. Paul reminds us, "Each of you should look not only to your own interest, but also to the interests of others" (v. 4). He encouraged the Philippians (and us) to consider the attitude of Christ Jesus, who humbled Himself to death on a cross (v. 8)!

God provides many opportunities to practice an attitude of humility and service or to offer an encouragement to someone who looks sad. However, we are often selfish and self-centered and don't notice someone who needs kind words.

> **Today's Peace Step**
> Allow your attitude
> and words to
> be filled with
> humility and love.

More often than not, we fail to cheer on those around us, and we crave attention and praise for ourselves. But our goal should be to follow Christ and show love.

He Cried for Help! (Biblical Story)

"How long, LORD, must I call for help . . ." HABAKKUK 1:2 *(NIV)*

Have you ever wondered why evil sometimes seems to triumph? Habakkuk did. Does it seem that corrupt men often go unpunished? Habakkuk thought so.

Habakkuk lived during a time when Judah, the northern kingdom of Israel, experienced moral and spiritual decline. Powerful and unholy neighbors threatened them. Their situation became so dire that Habakkuk cried out, "How long, LORD, must I call for help?"

God's answer may have seemed strange to Habakkuk. God called him to be patient. In time, the greedy and selfish people would destroy themselves. One day (in God's timing) the evil ones would be scorned and shamed, never to rise again, and the neighboring country Chaldea would conquer them. This caused the prophet to complain again because he understood God would let an evil nation conquer Judah.

God assured Habakkuk that the evil conquerors would also be punished at the right time. God didn't tell Habakkuk when all of this would happen, but he did develop Habakkuk's trust. The prophet realized God heard his cries and answered him. He found peace through trust in God, and faith to rejoice in God's sovereignty even in such an evil time.

Today's Peace Step

Trust God in
the midst of
difficult times.

At the end of the book of Habakkuk, he praised God: "Though the fig tree does not bud and there are no grapes on the vines, though the olive crop fails, and the fields produce no food, though there are no sheep in the pen and no cattle in the stalls, yet I will rejoice in the Lord, I will be joyful in God my Savior" (3:17–18, NIV).

The apostle Paul quoted Habakkuk in some of his letters because the people in Paul's day paralleled the people in the times of the prophet. We live in a difficult time too. Choose to trust God as He provides for your every need now and throughout the future. Choose to peacefully wait for God to act.

Remaining Fruitful

I am the vine; you are the branches. If you remain in me and I in you, you will bear much fruit; apart from me you can do nothing." JOHN 15:5 (NIV)

A history-making operation was performed on a daring twelve-year-old boy a few years ago. Everett Knowles chose to do something wrong. The red-headed, freckle-faced boy chose to hook a ride on a train in Boston. He successfully grabbed a ride on a slow-moving freight train and held on to the handrail, enjoying the breeze. But tragedy struck. His body slammed into a concrete overpass and abutment and severed his right arm, which he used as a Little League pitcher. Thankfully, the arm somehow remained in the sleeve and police rushed him to a Boston hospital. Eddy asked the doctor, "Can you save it?"

Space will not permit a lengthy description of the operation, but Dr. Ronald A. Malt painstakingly sewed the critical brachial arteries and veins in place, one at a time, to restore circulation. As he worked the hospital chaplain prayed and gave him last rites. They were also able to rejoin the severed humerus bone and later the other nerves in Everett's arm. They watched him carefully for infection, but he remained healthy.

> **Today's Peace Step**
> Ask God to daily remind you of your need for Him.

Everett survived and as an adult enjoyed weightlifting and tennis. The doctors who performed the miraculous procedure blazed a new trail in medicine.

This dramatic story illustrates Christ's analogy of the vine and the branches. If an arm must remain in the body to receive a proper blood supply, so a Christian must remain, or abide, in the Savior to produce fruit.

Only as we remain in Christ can we expect to see development in the areas of gentleness and humility, even when we are experiencing a sudden or a long-standing struggle.

Bearing Fruit (Historic Story)

But the fruit of the Spirit is love, joy, peace, forbearance, kindness, goodness, faithfulness, gentleness and self-control.
GALATIANS *5:22–23 (NIV)*

Benjamin's mother asked him to watch his younger sister, Sally. To occupy his time, and also wanting to surprise her, Benjamin set out to paint Sally's picture. Needless to say, a young boy and paint can be a problem, and soon he splattered the messy liquid everywhere.

However, this time Benjamin was the one surprised because when his mother returned she made no mention of the havoc. Instead, she stooped down, kissed him on the cheek, and exclaimed, "Oh, Benjamin, it's Sally!"

> **Today's Peace Step**
> Use your talents
> to share faith
> and beauty.

American artist, Benjamin West, said this one event launched his career. Instead of demonstrating an attitude of self-absorption and disgust, his mother put love for her child ahead of herself. She demonstrated joy in embracing her son, peace and self-control in remaining calm amid a

GROWING A PEACEFUL HEART

mess, patience with her children, kindness with her words, and gentleness with her kiss! She also showed faithfulness as a mom and child of God with her words that encouraged his career.

Benjamin, a self-taught artist, became famous for his historic paintings such as *Peace Treaty of Paris* and religious paintings of biblical scenes such as *Revealed Religion*, which included Christ healing the sick, Moses receiving the Ten Commandments, Paul's surviving the shipwreck at Malta, and Noah after the flood. He was raised in a Quaker community and learned about pigments from Native Americans. Although born in Pennsylvania, he moved to England and served as the official painter for King George III and a founder of the Royal Academy.

Such attributes are named as a gift from the Holy Spirit. Abraham Kuyper once wrote, "To be near unto God requires constant and continuous communication with our source of strength and salvation." God blesses us with these wonderful attributes when we let the Holy Spirit guide our lives.

Hair and Heart Care

When doubts filled my mind, your comfort gave me renewed hope and cheer. PSALM 94:19 (NLT)

Going to the beauty shop was, at the least, a distraction from Sara's current concerns. Having recently learned that her daughter needed surgery, she worried about her and what might be ahead for the future.

Her beautician was finishing up with her other customer, so she suggested Sara let her assistant shampoo her to save some time. Sara always enjoyed chatting with the assistant, a very pleasant person and good listener. That day, however, Sara found it hard to smile and join in their usual banter. She sat numb and a bit glum.

It appeared that Rena sensed Sara's worry, because she asked, "Are you okay?"

"Well, I suppose so, but . . ."

At this point, Sara didn't go into detail but mentioned that her daughter's upcoming surgery. Rena knew all about Sara's family from past chats and understood how much each daughter meant to Sara. Rena had also shared information about her own children.

"Well, then," Rena smiled, "this shampoo can wait."

With that, she took Sara's hand and led her to the back of the room. Then she put her arm around her and began to softly sing "What a Friend We Have in Jesus." The verse that spoke to Sara the most was "Are we weak and heavy laden, Cumbered with a load of care? Precious Savior, still our refuge—Take it to the Lord in prayer."

> **Today's Peace Step**
> When worries invade your heart, talk to Jesus.

Sara relaxed in Rena's arms and felt embraced by Jesus and a sense of peace for the rest of the day. She hugged Rena. She left the beauty parlor, after getting her hair done, with a smile.

BECOMING PEACEMAKERS

The Christian needs to walk in peace, so no matter what happens they will be able to bear witness to a watching world.
—HENRY BLACKABY

Once we have inner peace and learn to live in peace and develop healthy relationships, we can reach out to more people to share the peace of Christ and how to be at peace. Choose each morning to pray, forgive, bless others, and put others first and you will become a peacemaker.

Week 25

Peace with the Community and World

A Prayer to Appreciate Others

Oh Lord, may we praise you for being the Prince of Peace. We have done nothing to earn your love, recognition, or acceptance. You love everyone and make each person unique. You carefully fashioned us all in your image.

We do not appreciate your creativity in making people enough. We tend to spurn others who look or behave differently from us. We are especially reluctant to accept people from other cultures or who have different faith beliefs.

Sometimes we try to excuse ourselves by saying we are too busy or that other matters are more important. Often our decisions are based on selfishness and pride. Help us to know you have a purpose for the people you put in our lives, and keep our eyes open to their needs and our calling.

Help us love everyone and see the image of you in them. Help us be peacemakers who reach out to understand and value differences. Let us see into the hearts of people and know their need for love and rejoice in people who love like you do.

Wisdom from Young Peacemakers

Flowers and people are all different. That makes the world more interesting.

We can have peace by being kind to one another.

Continuing the Journey (Historic Story)

He saved us, not on the basis of deeds which we did in righteousness, but in accordance with His mercy, by the washing of regeneration and renewing by the Holy Spirit. TITUS 3:5

We can emulate God's compassion we see in other Christians. In World War II, fifteen-year-old Charles Brown, a West Virginia farm boy, served as a pilot on his first combat mission. After being shot to pieces by swarming German fighters, his plane flew alone in the skies above Germany. Half his crew lay wounded, the tail gunner lay dead, and his blood seemed frozen in icicles over the machine guns. Suddenly, the pilot glanced outside his cockpit and froze.

Staring at the same horrible vision, his copilot said, "My God, this is a nightmare."

The two men watched a gray German Messerschmitt fighter hover three feet off their wingtip. Only five days before Christmas 1943, this German pilot appeared to be closing in for the kill.

At this point, something strange occurred. When Brown and his copilot, Spencer "Pinky" Luke, looked again, the German didn't pull the trigger. Instead, he nodded and motioned for Brown to follow him. What happened next is now considered one of the most remarkable acts of chivalry of the war. The German pilot led his opponent to safety, and later Brown tracked down the man who showed mercy. Their reunion brought them both to tears.

> **Today's Peace Step**
> Instead of anger, show mercy.

God has every reason for anger toward us because of our sins. However, He delights in mercy. Becoming a Christian involves a total change, a new mind desiring to please God in thoughts, words, and actions. As believers, God the Holy Spirit continues His work in us. Our calling is to allow God to lead, guide, and strengthen us every day. When we show mercy we will also reveal a path to peace and a way to build relationships.

Caring or Chaos

Do to others as you would have them do to you. LUKE 6:31 *(NIV)*

Could it be an earthquake? How else could you explain the loud boom? Daylan McLee's house in Uniontown, Pennsylvania, began to shake as they held a family Father's Day picnic. Suddenly, a relative rushed inside to say a car had just crashed outside Daylan's house.

McLee, an African American, ran outside to find two cars had crashed, with Officer Jay Hanley inside the mangled patrol car. Hanley said the accident injured his leg and he didn't want to be moved, but then the car burst into flames. Flames started to come inside the patrol car, so McLee ripped the door off and started to drag Hanley out of the vehicle. Bystanders stated that Daylan appeared to have Herculean strength. Medics airlifted Hanley to the hospital. The other driver that collided with Hanley walked to the ambulance.

All of this happened during protests over police brutality following the death of George Floyd in Minneapolis.

Tensions were high, but Daylan McLee saw an immediate need and moved to save a life. Daylan confessed that he did not have the best past with law enforcement, but he stated, "There is value in every human life. We are all children of God, and I can't imagine just watching anyone burn." Daylan had spent a year in prison under false charges until a jury reviewed security footage and acquitted him. His sense of mercy outweighed any anger from the injustice.

McLee realized later that he had met Hanley while the officer patrolled their area. He knew Hanley to be friendly and that he never harassed anyone. He was truly a *peace* officer.

> **Today's Peace Step**
>
> We cannot see into the future, but we can stay in constant contact with God and ask Him to direct our every action.

Later, the police chief himself contacted McLee to thank him for his bravery, as did several members of Hanley's family. Caring should always conquer chaos.

Who Is My Neighbor? (Biblical Story)

Love your enemies and pray for those who persecute you, that you may be children of your Father in heaven. MATTHEW *5:44–45 (NIV)*

Dangerous things can happen on desolate roads. This was certainly true when robbers attacked, stripped, robbed a man, and then left him to die on a lonely road between Jerusalem and Jericho.

Jesus continued this story by saying that a Jewish priest later approached this victim but quickly ignored him and hurried away.

Later, another man of a priestly family, a Levite, came along, and he, too, ignored him and scurried by.

Finally, a Samaritan man, hated by the Jews, came along, and showed pity for the man. The Samaritan poured oil and wine on the wounds and bandaged them. He took the injured man to an inn and cared for him. The next day he gave the innkeeper two days' wages to provide for him and said he would return to pay whatever more might be needed.

Why did Jesus tell this story? Jesus had been teaching the way to eternal life. One day a scribe, a lawyer whose job was to copy and interpret the law approached Him, and asked, "What must I do to inherit eternal life?"

A discussion followed in which Jesus pointed out that the man needed to love God and his neighbor (Luke 10:25–27).

When the scribe asked, "Who is my neighbor?" Jesus told the story of the Good Samaritan and then asked, "Which one of the three travelers proved to be a neighbor?"

> **Today's Peace Step**
> We are busy and preoccupied, but find ways to show mercy every day.

The lawyer replied, "The one who showed mercy." He realized that our actions and mercy reveal our relationship with others.

Jesus then said, "Go and do the same." It's a lesson for all people to realize that anyone in need of mercy is our neighbor. We are called to heal wounds and hearts to bring peace.

But What About Today?

Now if we are children, then we are heirs—heirs of God and co-heirs with Christ, if indeed we share in his sufferings in order that we may also share in his glory. ROMANS 8:17 (NIV)

Who said, "These are the times that try men's souls . . . ? It was Thomas Paine who wrote this line in "The American Crises" in December 1776.

Today, we face a world crisis. In fact, our present upheaval is unlike anything the world has ever seen. Covid-19 and all its variants are attacking our bodies, minds, emotions, and finances.

What are we to think and do? First, we should remind ourselves this is no surprise to God. If He called Christ to suffer in order to save us, surely we may be called to suffer for our spiritual growth. Our second call is to trust and rely on God's strength. This alone can make us stand under our load of affliction and have peace in the midst of chaos.

Thirdly, we should consider how our life is preparing us to rejoice in heaven. After we have lived on earth amid evil and pain, we will be welcomed into God's presence. He will wipe away every tear from our eyes. That is when we will share in God's glory, as today's verse mentions. That reminds us that sometimes we are called to share in suffering. We live in a fallen world where people choose to do evil, and scientists play with germs that can cause great harm.

We can choose to act in peace. We can share goods in short supply rather than hoarding. We can show compassion to those who are sick. We can give gener-

ously, or even out of our own need, to help others. We can be positive and comforting to lift the spirits of those who live in fear.

On earth we need to trust our days and lives to God.

A Surprise Encounter (Historic Story)

So then you are no longer strangers and aliens, but you are fellow citizens with the saints and members of the household of God, built on the foundation of the apostles and prophets, Christ Jesus himself being the cornerstone, in whom the whole structure, being joined together, grows into a holy temple in the Lord. EPHESIANS 2:19–21 (ESV)

Dr. R. C. Sproul told a story about an incident on a train a number of years ago when he and his wife, Vesta, were traveling in Hungary. The train rolled along between stops. At one point an official boarded the train and asked for their papers. After a quick look and a nod, he then demanded they open their suitcases. Sproul felt a bit nervous when the intruder stared at the object sitting on the top of his clothing: a Bible.

The official glared at the Bible and then into Sproul's face. "Are you a Christian?" he demanded.

"Yes, I am," Sproul confessed.

A period of silence followed, and then the officer said, "Well, so am I!" Then, before Sproul could react, he continued, "Are you a citizen of the United States?"

"Yes, I am."

Another brief silence and then the officer rebuked him. "No, first and foremost, we are citizens of heaven."

Relieved, Sproul smiled, and the two men shook hands, knowing they were no longer strangers and aliens, but fellow citizens with the saints on earth and in heaven. What peace to meet another Christian! It's true. The kingdom of God is international without borders. Our purpose is to continue to grow in our faith and for us to invite more people to know Christ and increase the kingdom of God.

> **Today's Peace Step**
>
> Always be willing and ready to share the joy of heaven with anyone God puts in your path.

Letting others know we are Christians builds bridges with other Christians and provides opportunities for unbelievers to hear about God. Once they hear they can seek God and choose to become Christians.

Week 26

Seeking Peace

Prayer to Seek Peace

Lord, help me seek ways to love others with different views and different perspectives on politics, faith, morality, and other issues. May your Holy Spirit guide us all to truth that will unite us. Meanwhile, help us show kindness and speak gently when we share our opinions.

Keep me from preaching. Let my life show others the difference being a Christian makes in me. Let your stories and your Word teach us all. May we act in kindness daily, sit together at the same table, and break bread while trusting you to love us and bring us together in peace.

May we praise peacemakers and strive to bring peace to people around us.

Wisdom from Young Peacemakers

Go outside. Trees and fresh air make people nicer.

If we play together, we can become friends.

Getting Together Amid Family Difference

Finally, all of you, be like-minded, be sympathetic, love one another, be compassionate and humble. 1 PETER 3:8 (NIV)

The past few years have been tough on families. One family fights over politics while another fights over faith. Still others have to deal with difficult personalities—attention grabber, whiner, over-sharer, busybody, bully, gossip, and so on. Each family needs to set some boundaries to handle the stress of relationships and differing opinions. Keep the focus on love.

Marie's family makes holidays big game days with tables, chairs, and lots of board games. Candy's family polls people and decides on a movie for the grownups and one for the kids. When we are busy and focused, it's harder to argue.

Other families, like Ben's gang, set a few boundaries like no talk about politics, faith, age, or weight. If someone starts to, they need to put a dollar in the fight pot that will later be given to charity (they draw the name of who chooses the recipient).

> **Today's Peace Step**
> The best peace step is to choose to add joy and avoid arguing.

Steve starts his family off by greeting each person at the door, asking for the individual to name a blessing, and posting the blessings. That helps people share and focus on positive ideas. We can also dodge the bullets of mean comments with a gracious response like, "It's not part of today's conversation," or "We all have our problems, but we don't need to air them

GROWING A PEACEFUL HEART

when we want to celebrate!" Or we can switch gossip to an opportunity to consider how to help the person, pause and pray, show compassion, and be sympathetic.

Whatever your family does, you can be a peacemaker by encouraging the people around you and deflecting the negative comments by ignoring them or asking how you can help. Sprinkle in joy with extra little gifts for kids and the host or hostess. Add lots of hugs and compliments.

Abigail Peacemaker (Biblical Story)

Turn from evil and do good; seek peace and pursue it. PSALM *34:14 (NIV)*

Abigail's servant raced to share the bad news that her husband, Nabal, had rejected David's request for food. David and his men protected Nabal's land, so Nabal's response angered David and he prepared to fight.

Abigail responded immediately to the news by loading donkeys with two hundred loaves of bread, five sheep, a hundred cakes of raisins, two hundred fig cakes, and more. She proceeded to meet David and his men. She bowed before David and asked that her gifts be given to his men. She pleaded with him to not be burdened with needless bloodshed, especially because he was Israel's future king. David agreed.

Abigail understood the pride of men and how to appease them. She took control of the mess her foolish husband created. She approached David humbly and spoke kindly. She sought forgiveness for her husband's offense and for her role as a mediator in trying to prevent a disaster and save the lives of the servants in her home. She put the needs of people before herself. God gifted her with wisdom and beauty that she used to calm David.

Abigail understood her husband although she did not agree with him. She risked her life to give food to David and his men, knowing her husband could kill her for her actions. She didn't hide what she did and told her husband about all her actions. The next morning God caused Nabal's heart to turn to stone, and he died. David praised God for taking care of his enemy Nabal and then asked Abigail to marry him. She accepted.

> **Today's Peace Step**
> When you see a way to help bring peace, act on the idea.

God protected Abigail and avenged David [Her story is in 1 Samuel 25]. Like Abigail, we can respond to disputes with action to help bring peace.

Grocery Store Kindness by Melissa Henderson

Pleasant words are a honeycomb, sweet to the soul and healing to the bones. PROVERBS *16:24*

Melissa waited patiently in line at the local grocery store. The store had recently shortened the hours of operation due to lack of staff. In the past, there would have been five checkout lines open. Today, only one person worked at a register. Not even a bagger.

As Melissa waited, she began thinking about the frazzled employee, sweat running down her face while rushing to scan groceries and then place the items in bags.

The customer in front of Melissa never said a word to the employee. After his transaction was completed, he grabbed his items and left.

Melissa moved forward to have her turn checking out. She smiled and said, "Good morning. Looks like you are busy today. Thank you for being here."

The cashier paused and looked at Melissa as tears pooled in her blue eyes. "Thank you, ma'am. No one hardly ever speaks to me. Most people are mad about the wait. I appreciate your smile and your kindness."

As Melissa continued to chat with the cashier while items were scanned and bagged, a peace came over the line of customers. Melissa noticed the once tapping feet behind her had stopped. A few customers began thanking the employee for working and helping keep the store open. The people in line also replaced frowns with smiles, and a few started talking.

A peace that only God could have provided came over that part of the store. For a few minutes in the day, peace came through words, kindness, and encouragement. After Melissa observed

> **Today's Peace Step**
> Share the peace of God by having a conversation with a store employee.

the contagiousness of kindness in action, she resolved to encourage workers more often.

Winston Churchill's V Sign (Historic Story)

Surely you need guidance to wage war, and victory is won through many advisers. PROVERBS 24:6 (NIV)

On July 19, 1941, at one of Britain's lowest points of World War II, Churchill launched the V for victory campaign. Holding up two fingers to form a V was not new during this war, but Churchill made great use of it to inspire hope.

His radio address that day included these words: "The V sign is the symbol of the unconquerable will of the occupied territories and a portent of the fate awaiting Nazi tyranny. So long as the peoples continue to refuse all collaboration with the invader it is sure his cause will perish, and that Europe will be liberated." Soon the sign appeared on walls and other places, and people tapped the 'V' in Morse code with knuckles, glasses, and pencils. The symbol became the rallying emblem for people suppressed under Hitler's occupation as they continued to resist, as well as throughout the free world as people stood in solidarity against the enemy.

A Belgian refugee named Victor de Laveleye served as an announcer on Radio Belgique during World War II. On January 14, 1941, he proposed the idea of using the V symbol that was the start of the Flemish and Dutch words for *freedom* as well as the English word for *victory*.

> **Today's Peace Step**
>
> Let the cross or other Christian symbol be your call for persistence in peace making.

He called on the listeners to write it everywhere, infinitely repeated. That message spread to France and eventually to England, where Colonel V. Britton shared it on his BBC broadcast. The *New York Times* picked up the news and called it a "unique nerve war against Germany."

The Morse code for V is three dots and a dash (. . . —) and that reflected the first notes of Beethoven's Fifth Symphony. The music became the theme song of Britton's program. Once Churchill used the symbol, it became his signature and went viral.

Peace Chair

Finally, brothers and sisters, whatever is true, whatever is noble, whatever is right, whatever is pure, whatever is lovely, whatever is admirable—if anything is excellent or praiseworthy—think about such things. PHILIPPIANS 4:8 (NIV)

Michelle got tired of her children whining and complaining. She wanted them to refocus and live in peace, so she decided to create a peace chair. She placed a comfy chair in a corner, added pretty pillows, and placed a basket next to it. She filled the basket with water, a few snacks, a Bible, and some squeeze balls. She added some index cards and colored pencils.

"Time to gather!" Michelle called, and the kids all came running. She shared that Jesus, the Prince of Peace, wants us to live in peace and not grumble. She explained she had a peace chair where she would send a whiny child, or anyone could ask for a turn in it if they needed to be calm or wanted a peace break. In the chair they could read the Bible and dwell on good thoughts. They could pray and tell God what bothered them and what made them smile.

They could also use a card to draw or write notes to thank God for blessings in their lives.

The children all clamored for a turn, so Michelle drew names and scheduled times for each to try it. She had no minimum time to be in the chair; she just suggested they remain in the chair until they felt peaceful or happy. They all liked their first turn. When Michelle had to send a child to the chair, they sometimes grumbled, but it worked. They had a quiet and safe place to calm down. They also laughed when Mom took a turn in the chair, but then they noticed it made her happier too when she had been yelling or upset.

> **Today's Peace Step**
> Create a peaceful spot to retreat and focus on God.

Dad used the chair when he came home after a stressful day, and that helped the children give him a little time alone. When he got up he would smile and play.

Little Randy said, "I like our peace chair. It changes grumps to grins."

Week 27

Peace after War

Prayer for Peace from Wars

Dear Father, war tears us apart and hurts so many people. Bless warriors with inner peace when they return home. Comfort the family members of those who serve that they may not fear.

Beyond wars with countries, help us with the battles in our homes. When we reconcile, help us have peace in our hearts and peace between those who were involved.

Lord, be the peacemaker to stop the aggression of strong nations toward weaker nations. Protect the lives of innocent children, the aged, and civilians.

Let us use our time to love and cherish one another instead of arguing and hurting one another. Let us be united through you. After peace treaties and settled disputes, may we be generous and nurturing to those who opposed us. May we forgive and plant seeds of peace.

Wisdom from Young Peacemakers

If we take off our skin, we are all the same.

We need to grow more food so people will be happy and not fight anymore.

Fort Garden

And He will judge between the nations, and will mediate for many peoples; and they will beat their swords into plow-shares, and their spears into pruning knives. Nation will not lift up a sword against nation, and never again will they learn war. ISAIAH 2:4

During the American Revolution, cannons mounted behind sixteen-inch-thick brick walls stood firm on a small island, to fire on approaching enemies. The tiny island, known as Governor's Island, sits in the New York Harbor. In the 1980s, when Rebecca and her family lived there, they gardened in the space between the walls and cannon turrets, the old mounts where cannons had once stood. Two-feet-wide sections of soil lay between the wall and each mount.

As crops ripened, the produce grew large. Carrots grew several inches long and about five inches in diameter. Cucumbers grew as long as two feet. The produce blossomed through the end of November. The brick wall heated up during the day and kept the plants warm at night. No one had planted in the soil for so long that it was rich and full of nutrients. The place that had seen war during the American Revolution now produced nourishment. They filled baskets with fresh vegetables and gave much away, especially to friends who lived in apartments. School children on the

> **Today's Peace Step**
> Grow a plant or garden as a reminder to pray for peace.

GROWING A PEACEFUL HEART

island took field trips in the fall to the pumpkin patch in the garden, and they played on the grass.

One black cannon remained in the back yard, outside the kitchen door, where up to seven children climbed, played, and picnicked. The children sat on the cannon as they munched on the fresh produce. They also could stand and see the World Trade Center that terrorists attacked and destroyed a decade later. Scripture promises that one day all weapons will be transformed with reshaping into tools to grow produce.

Saul from Destroyer to Peacemaker Paul (Biblical Story)

Yet for this reason I found mercy, so that in me as the foremost sinner Jesus Christ might demonstrate His perfect patience as an example for those who would believe in Him for eternal life. 1 TIMOTHY 1:16

Saul's anger and hatred caused him to seek out believers to kill them. He continued his rage and fight until Christ stopped him with a bolt of lightning (Acts 9) and said, "I am Jesus whom you are persecuting." Saul discovered that in hurting anyone he hurt Jesus.

Battles and wars often begin in the heart. God is the one who can change hearts. God's love and truth replaced Saul's anger. When God changed Saul, Ananias and others felt fearful until God calmed their fears. The change amazed people, but as God had told Ananias Saul became an instrument for God and an instrument of peace.

He took on his Roman name of Paul, meaning "small," for he understood that God is the one who is great. Paul began his letters with a greeting of grace and peace from God the Father, and Christ. As a Jew, he understood that *shalom* for peace meant "well-being" and "wholeness." God can give us peace and lasting change in our hearts that results in peaceful choices and actions.

> **Today's Peace Step**
> Soften your heart with forgiving everyone for any and all wrongs.

Paul's change did not end the persecution of Christians, and even now religious persecution continues. But Paul showed change is possible and how to stand firm in the face of oppression. His words still bring hope and remind us that Jesus shared that we are blessed when we are persecuted, and the reward is heaven.

Anger hardens hearts, as Paul knew from his days terrorizing believers. Forgiveness frees us and softens our hearts. Paul shared in Ephesians 4:32 that we should be tenderhearted and forgiving. That's what we need to achieve peace after war, within ourselves or with nations.

Japanese Peace Parks

The LORD will surely comfort Zion and will look with compassion on all her ruins; he will make her deserts like Eden, her wastelands like the garden of the LORD. Joy and gladness will be found in her, thanksgiving and the sound of singing. ISAIAH 51:3 (NIV)

Marjorie L. Mayer chose to serve as a missionary in Japan as World War II ended as part of a program called The Fellowship of Reconstruction. She and the others hoped to transform hearts and feelings of hate, distrust, and fear into ones of love, respect, and understanding. She and seven other young women taught Japanese girls near Nagasaki, the site of an atomic bombing.

Her students had experienced the horror and hopelessness of war and often spoke about faith, hope, and the meaning of life. Marjorie spent twenty-four years in Japan to bring reconciliation and hope to individuals she met. She observed the United States building their military to prevent another war while the Japanese built peace parks where bombs had exploded. Many of her students wanted to work for peace because their country was the only one to suffer a nuclear attack and radiation poisoning.

People created the Hiroshima Memorial Park over an open field made by the explosion. The Flame of Peace there is also a reminder of thousands of people who begged for water to quench their fever and sickness from the heat rays and fire that came with the bomb-

> **Today's Peace Step**
> Plant seeds of love today with your words and actions.

ing. The park is a tranquil space between two rivers where people can sit and reflect on peace. The annual ceremony held on August 6 includes 10,000 colored lanterns that contain peace prayers floating down the rivers.

God placed the first couple in a garden, a place of fruitfulness and beauty, a place where seeds grow and blossom to bring beauty and sweet fragrances. It's better to plant seeds of love and peace than to nurture anger and hatred.

John Stanley Grauel (Historic Story)

For the nation and the kingdom which will not serve you [Jerusalem] will perish, and the nations will be utterly ruined. ISAIAH 60:12

"It is my own deep conviction that the death of Israel would be the death knell of Western civilization." John worked hard to help Israel during World War II and persuaded the United Nations Special Committee on Palestine to recommend the Partition Resolution of 1947, creating the state of Israel. That returned land to Israel and gave them their sovereign country again. Golda Meir praised him for his assistance with her country's cause.

John's concern for Israel began as a child when his Christian mother championed the Israelites and their faith as the roots of the Christian faith. He became an ordained minister and married, but his wife and child died in childbirth. Photos in newspapers of Jews wearing the German Iron Cross for fighting for Germany in World War I while being forced to wash the streets of Berlin tore at his heart and motivated him to join the American Christian Palestine Committee to work to help Israel. John traveled to Israel and joined the Haganah underground with humanitarian efforts, including helping to free Jews in Europe.

He privately helped raise funds, bought guns and ammunition, and spoke publicly.

As the only non-Jew of the illegal immigrant ship *Warfield*, he played a pivotal role. The British had their ships ram the *Warfield*, determined to sink it and 4500 refugees if they did not surrender. British authorities arrested John and held him at the Savoy Hotel, where war cor-

Today's Peace Step
Pray for and support
all God's people,
including Jews.

respondents quickly sought him out. His testimony spread around the world. He continued sharing news with reporters and testified before the United Nations. After the war ended, John spoke out to expose the mistreatment of Jews in Algeria and Morocco. Journalist Ruth Gruber renamed the ship the *Exodus*, the "Ship That Launched a Nation."

Peace from Post-Traumatic Stress

Moreover, I will give you a new heart and put a new spirit within you; and I will remove the heart of stone from your flesh and give you a heart of flesh. EZEKIEL 36:26

Suzy married, filled with love for her kind husband. She didn't know that he suppressed feelings and memories of seeing death daily as a marine, during the Vietnam War, until one night when he erupted like a volcano that pierced her heart. She felt she must have done something to hurt him.

Nothing she did kept away unexpected outbursts. Their children hid in closets, and she finally considered divorce. But, in her cry to God for help, she found Christ and prayed.

Phil thought he'd left the war and his work as a Marine machine gunner behind, but instead, he brought war into his home life. He grew up angry due to his father's adultery and the pain that caused his mother. After he found Christ, and men who had recovered from PTSD and who helped him and walked beside him, he slowly healed. Speaking about his feelings began his road to recovery. An accountability partner helped him change his actions to be a kinder and more loving individual and to deal with his anger and past struggles.

Today's Peace Step

When overwhelmed with stress or filled with fear from trauma, find a Christian who will listen, pray, and help you be accountable.

He became a speaker involved in various men's ministries to help other men find inner peace and restore relationships through methods of dealing with conflicts and techniques to soothe emotions. It's a process that Phil committed to work through daily to destress from trauma. He memorized Philippians 4:6–7 and other Scriptures and learned to take a moment as needed to ask God for help against stress and memories that flashed into his mind. He found that God will constantly give him peace and hope for every need, at every moment. He discovered that faith and dwelling on blessings pushes out the anger and other negative emotions.

Week 28

Peace with Respect

Prayer to Be More Respectful

Dear Lord, help us respect other people, especially ones who have different values and beliefs than our own. May we respond to people's remarks and questions with gentleness and honor. Let our words be uplifting and considerate even when we disagree. Let us remember that every individual is made in your image, God, and that you love everyone. Help us work to unite people and bring peace. Let me speak with love even when I share my own views and your words.

Help me show respect in my actions and guide me to treat each person with dignity. Help me see the beauty within a person's heart so I might respect him or her more. Help me encourage those around me to bring out the best in each person. Let me act with integrity so that others might respect me too.

Let respect bridge difference, and help us live in peace.

Wisdom from Young Peacemakers

UGH. I don't LIKE pizza. But if Grammy were here, I'd eat pizza because she loves pizza, and she doesn't get to eat it very much because Grandpa doesn't like cheese.

Dad used to yell in the car. Then he started saying a prayer when cars got in front of us. Prayer helps us have peace.

Freeing the Colors

He made from one man every nation of mankind to live on all the face of the earth, having determined their appointed times and the boundaries of their habitation. ACTS 17:26

Rebecca's dad showed her a prism and how she could see the colors within it when light passed through. She said, "Daddy, we're freeing the colors!"

A prism is a piece of glass in a triangular shape. When light passes through the glass, it slows down and then speeds up as it leaves the glass. When the light hits the glass at an angle, it bends or refracts. The colors within light travel at different speeds, and the prism helps split the light into those different colors. White light contains all the colors of the spectrum. Prisms make great optical tools. A lighthouse is able to shine a beam to a far distance because its small light is surrounded by prisms that intensify and focus the light source.

> **Today's Peace Step**
> Find a new quality within each person you interact with today.

Jesus called Himself the light of the world. In Him are all colors, and through Him all people of all colors were made. Love is what frees our hearts to love one another no matter the skin color. Seeing others through the lens of faith helps us find the best and live in peace with our neighbors. When we remain close to Jesus, we can reflect light and, like a prism, help show people the beauty within all the people God made. We can help people see and respect what's unseen.

Respect includes being sensitive to the feelings of others. That means considering our words so that we might not say something hurtful. This includes understanding and celebrating different cultures. It also means to see people like God does by looking within a person to his or her heart and not judging outward appearances. We free our hearts and relationships when we use Christ as our prism.

Nehemiah (Biblical Story)

"Please, give back to them this very day their fields, their vineyards, their olive groves, and their houses, as well as the hundredth part of the money and of the grain, the new wine, and the oil that you are charging as interest from them."
NEHEMIAH 5:11

The richer people took advantage of the poorer people through usury. They charged extraordinarily high interest. This outraged Nehemiah when he heard it. It caused great hardship among the poorer people because the practice forced their children into slavery.

As the governor, Nehemiah called an assembly and condemned the actions as shameful behavior. He reminded them they needed to fear God and be a better example to other nations. They needed to care for one another. They were all Israelites, all family.

The rich people agreed and listened to Nehemiah. They returned fields, vineyards, homes, and a portion of interest paid. Nehemiah, their leader, set a great example.

Nehemiah knew the leaders before him taxed the people and took a food allowance to increase their wealth and pay their entertainment expenses. He showed great love for the people by not placing burdens on them. He daily fed visiting Jews and dignitaries with his own money and supplies. He also knew the people had been restoring the wall around Jerusalem with him, unable to work their own businesses, and respected their situation.

Restoration of possessions restored relationships and brought peace among the people. God wants us to have compassion and treat people fairly, as we want to be treated. Democracy allows us to show respect for all people by making fair lending laws that helps people avoid loan sharks, who take advantage of someone's hardships. It can be easy, as an individual, to take advantage of someone and let another person do more of the work or to continually drop by someone's home, eat there, and let them spend money to feed you.

> **Today's Peace Step**
> Choose to be generous and treat others with compassion.

Driver's Test

Respect everyone and show special love for God's people. Honor God and respect the Emperor. 1 PETER 2:17 CEV

Karen showed up for her driver's test and met the man conducting the exam. She did fine with driving straight, taking turns, and backing up. She followed the laws and stayed in her lane. Then the examiner asked her to parallel park her parents' large sedan behind a very small car.

Her first attempt had her too far into the driving lane. Her second had her at an angle with the hood sticking into the road. The examiner kept nagging her and telling her what to do, causing stress. Finally, she stopped, put on the brake, turned to the examiner, and said, "Please be quiet and let me try again. I may not be perfect, and I will walk a mile or more if needed when there's no close and easy parking space, until I get better, but I can't do this with a passenger who is adding stress."

The man became silent. Karen took off the brake and tried again. She did okay but not perfect, sighed, and said, "Thanks for letting me do it one more time." He then directed her to return to the motor vehicle department. She thought, *I imagine I failed, but at least I am calm. I can try again.*

When she parked, the examiner gave her a paper and said, "You passed. Go get your license." Her jaw dropped, and she stared at him.

He said, "Anyone who can politely tell an examiner to be quiet will do okay on the road. You know enough to remain calm and take your time. That helps keep the roads safe."

> **Today's Peace Step**
> Remember to be respectful even under stress or pressure.

The pass surprised her driver's ed teacher, who had never had a student pass with that examiner on their first try. No matter the pressure or our circumstances, respect can make a difference.

Prince Albert (Historic Story)

They only asked us to remember the poor—the very thing I also was eager to do. GALATIANS 2:10

Prince Albert, husband of Queen Victoria, called his bride an angel sent from heaven whose brightness would bring light into his life. The two loved each other deeply, and that love spilled over into caring for people. Albert strove to make life better for all people. He campaigned for social reforms. He encouraged the building of new houses for working people with better ventilation and improved sanitation. He tried to improve the welfare pensions for servants and education for all children, and promoted benevolent societies and the generosity of wealthier people to help the poor. Albert spoke at The Society for Extinction of the Slave Trade and for the Civilization of Africa, labeling slavery a stain on civilized Europe.

He and the queen understood violence but advocated for peace. They survived several assassination attempts, including one they encountered as they rode in a carriage in 1840. Victoria commuted the death of the assassin's sentence to banishment for life. Albert looked for ways to show respect and concern for all people and to work for social justice and peace.

He believed machinery and science belonged to the civilized world, not one country. He organized the Great Exhibition to showcase technology and new ideas, including the best of British technology. He built the Crystal Palace to house the international event and its 100,000 exhibits. Close to six million people visited the exhibit.

Meant to promote peace, the exhibit served as the first place where nations of the world came together off the battlefield. Historian Asa Briggs referred to the palace as a temple of peace.

Albert also enjoyed music. He played the organ and composed at least forty pieces of music, including church hymns. He asked for

> **Today's Peace Step**
> Act on your desires to help people in need.

his favorite hymn, "Rock of Ages," to be sung at his death-bed, revealing his faith and hope in Christ.

Road Rage

"In everything, therefore, treat people the same way you want them to treat you, for this is the Law and the Prophets." MATTHEW 7:12

Jim listened to the driver curse another car as it cut them off. He said, "You don't know what's happening in the life of that driver. Why, he might even be having a heart attack." The other car slowed, and the driver slumped over. They stopped and Jim got out. The other driver did have a heart attack. No one in the carpool complained about other drivers again. They were all more gracious to drivers and signaled for others to come over if they saw a turn signal on.

Jim went a little further. He began praying when a driver cut him, drove too slowly, or passed too close. He prayed for the other driver. He considered that God put the person in his path because that person needed prayer.

It replaced anger with a purpose, a call from God to be kinder in his thoughts and words.

After a disaster hit his area, he noticed people driving crazier than in the past. He realized they could not focus well, as he watched drivers swerve more within their lanes and cross into the shoulder at times. The lack of electricity that caused traffic lights not to work added to the confusion. When workers mentioned the crazy drivers, he reminded them that the disaster caused many problems including shock and difficulty coping with the rubble and brokenness around them.

Today's Peace Step

Pray when strangers act carelessly or anger you.

People often react without understanding. Yes, many times someone purposely cuts in front of another car, but that person is often angry and in pain. They really need prayer. They need someone to care and extend grace. Prayer also calms our emotions, decreases anger, and helps us focus on God's call to love, be kinder, and pray for others.

Week 29

Peacemakers

Prayer to Be a Peacemaker

Lord, help me be a peacemaker. Let me forgive, and show kindness and respect toward all people. Help me listen attentively with my heart. Help me understand and respond to people's different views with love. Let me share my faith and view with love.

May I be the first to reach out to forgive. May I pause before I speak, watch for opportunities to help people in need, and always show respect to everyone I meet.

Forgive me when I fail and burst out in anger or try to get my own way that can cause hurt and divide people rather than unite them. Guide me to be a peacemaker and to bridge the gap between people. Let me build bridges or understanding where there are gaps of anger. Let me be unafraid to help solve conflicts.

Wisdom from Young Peacemakers

I can be less annoying. My sister doesn't like it when I move too much.

If we are happy inside, then we won't argue and fight.

Putting Other First

Do not merely look out for your own personal interests, but also for the interests of others. PHILIPPIANS *2:4*

Jim lost his mother at a young age. His father, an immigrant and long shoreman, could not cope with his young children and placed them in an orphanage. Jim longed to get out and often sneaked into the chapel to plead for God to give him a new home. God not only left him there, but when Jim reached age eighteen, God called him to become a priest. At first he cried, "No," but gradually realized that was his path.

His first assignment was in an asylum. He felt he'd been in institutions for so long but chose to take a positive outlook. One of the first patients he served was a former nun who used all her strength to be mean. He didn't know much about her since his superiors wanted him to look at each person with fresh eyes through the lens of prayer.

He sat beside the woman and began talking. She glared at him and then leaned over to purposefully vomit on him. She stared at him. He took out a handkerchief and looked at it and then looked at her. He then leaned over and began wiping off her face. A tear trickled down her cheek, followed by more tears. When she was healed she told him that he began the healing. He was the first person who had ever put her first and cared for her needs before their own needs.

> **Today's Peace Step**
> Put someone
> else first.

It doesn't take a huge gesture or plan to make a difference or be a peacemaker. One simple action to love another person can change a life. A moment to bless someone with kindness or encouragement can change their day or even their outlook. Whether Jesus hugged one child, fed thousands, or healed one person, he touched lives and changed how people thought and acted. Pray each morning for an opportunity to bring peace, and then act on that prayer at each opportunity to bring peace into someone's life.

Isaac's Well (Biblical Story)

Then he moved away from there and dug another well, and they did not quarrel over it; so he named it Rehoboth, for he said, "At last the has made room for us, and we will be fruitful in the land." GENESIS 26:22

Isaac's new neighbors in Gerar continually made trouble for him. He would dig a well, and herdsmen would want it. He let them have the wells. Isaac had moved to the land because of a famine. God told him to stay there and promised to bless him.

Isaac lived in the valley of Gerar where Abraham dwelled at one time. He dug up the old wells Abraham had dug and used the same names for them. The local herdsmen quarreled over the wells and claimed them. Isaac changed the well's name to "contention," and another he named "enmity." Digging wells meant hard work in hot, dry land. Finally, at the third well he dug with his servants, no one quarreled. He named that one "broad places" as a reminder that God made room for him and his people.

Once Isaac settled by the new well, God appeared to him and blessed him again. Afterward, Abimelech, a leader from Gerar who hated Isaac, came to Isaac. Isaac questioned why he came. Abimelech explained that he had seen God's blessing on Isaac and wanted to make peace. They made a covenant and celebrated with a feast. At the end of the celebration his servants came and announced they had dug another well and found water.

Today's Peace Step

Trust God to be your path to peace.

Isaac never fought back but kept moving away. He trusted God would direct him to a place of peace. For Isaac, the quarrels and disputes seemed to be an indicator that those places were not God's plan for him. He lived according to his faith, and others noticed. God's blessing on Isaac caused his enemies to want peace. God, the greatest peacemaker, changes hearts and minds.

Grandma's Loaves

And he would answer and say to them, "The one who has two tunics is to share with the one who has none; and the one who has food is to do likewise." LUKE 3:11

Karen asked her grandma why she always baked at least two loaves of bread since her mother only made one at a time and they had a larger family in her home.

Grandma said, "Two loaves are better than one. There's always someone who needs a loaf of bread." She showed Karen the calendar she kept in her purse. She pointed out circled dates that reminded her of people who lost a loved one months earlier. She said, "Many people forget how someone grieving misses the person they loved and that kindness from someone helps them feel better." She made a loaf of bread to give people months after the death.

That day she planned to give the extra bread to someone new in town. She also had a few little toys to give their children. Karen went along with her grandma and met the new family. She played with the little girl. As they drove back to Grandma's house, Karen said, "I made a new friend. They're not just strangers in town anymore because we know them."

Grandma smiled and said, "Yes, I like meeting people and welcoming them. That helps us make this community more friendly."

Later that day Karen and her grandma knitted doll clothes. Karen said, "I can make doll clothes for you to give other new children who move here or who have lost someone they love.

Grandma smiled and replied, "That's a good idea. I'll buy a few dolls. We'll keep them handy for a child who needs them." The doorbell rang, and Karen ran to welcome in the visitor.

The lady gave Grandma cookies to thank her for bringing her bread when she moved in. Grandma said, "Karen, this is another new person in town. Sharing grows a good community."

> **Today's Peace Step**
> Make friends with one person or family at a time.

Mr. Rogers (Historic Story)

Love does no wrong to a neighbor; therefore love is the fulfillment of the Law. ROMANS 13:10

Fred Rogers started with a neighborhood to share ways to live in peace. His puppet neighborhood showed children how to settle problems and respond to difficult people, like King Friday's attempt to put a barbed wire around his home. The citizens sent him messages in balloons to show their views.

He closed the show by stating, "I like you as you are." Those words encouraged children and helped them to work at liking other people with different personalities and interests. He modeled respect and good listening skills. He invited people from his imaginary world into his home, the set of the show, to talk. Guests included a handicapped boy whose family had written to him, a marine biologist, a famous chef, a jazz trumpeter, and the regulars such as the delivery man Mr. McFeely, Emily the poetry lady, and Officer Clemmons.

> **Today's Peace Step**
> Be a friendly
> neighbor who
> listens to everyone
> you meet.

His gentle nature and openness to talk about anything helped children become peacemakers. In real life, Fred Rogers was the same as seen on his show, but it grew out of childhood challenges. He suffered from many illnesses, being overweight, and bullying. That developed empathy. He also had champions in family, friends, and other adults who encouraged him.

GROWING A PEACEFUL HEART

He became an ordained minister and TV producer. As an adult, he practiced kindness daily. He helped others and truly listened to people. He reminded people to be grateful by asking people to take a minute and think of someone who really helped them in their life.

Fred stayed in touch and encouraged many people with letters, cards, and calls. Communicating remains an important part of being a peacemaker. We need to follow Fred's example: listen and express respect in our tone as well as build bridges to what we have in common. He considered everyone a neighbor.

The Best Choice

In all things show yourself to be an example of good deeds, with purity in doctrine, dignified . . . Titus 2:7

John coached Little League baseball, and his team often won. One day, with the bleachers filled, John stopped the game. He walked over to the catcher on the other team and started directing the young boy on how to hold his glove and squat properly to catch better. Some of the parents of his players started yelling that he was helping the opponents.

John stood up, turned to the crowd, and explained that safety matters and the lad could get hurt because of his stance and the way he held the glove. The crowd stopped murmuring and clapped. The game resumed but with less heckling of the opposite teams and more cheering for good plays and hits. Both teams smiled at the end and gave players on the other team high fives and big smiles.

Few people recalled who won that day, but many people remembered the coach's example.

After the game, that young boy and his parents approached Coach John and thanked him for his sportsmanship and example. He tousled the boy's hair and said, "Keep practicing, and you'll make a great catcher."

When helping children, it's not about winning or losing as much as training young ones in how to do their best and how to be safe. Coaches who model caring for others also model peace and remind us that in games and life we should be watching out for the needs of others.

Today's Peace Step

Be an example by encouraging a game opponent or someone with different views.

God honors those people too, and when John retired from coaching the town named a new ball field after him.

Too often we let politics, cultures, or other differences divide us instead of reaching out to unite with others and work together to make life better for everyone.

Week 30

Praying for World Peace

Prayer for Lasting Peace

Almighty God, Creator of all people, help us to honor your name by showing cooperation and goodwill to other nations and cultures. Above all, may we share and live out the gospel so others might understand the way of grace and salvation.

By the power of the Holy Spirit, may we know and show others that even when peace is not abounding on the earth, it can, and will, remain in the hearts of those who know you. May we seek to be peacemakers and prayer warriors.

Help us to be calm, to show love, and to continue to pray for peace.

Wisdom from Young Peacemakers

We can have peace in this world when everyone believes in God.

We all need to be nice and kind and make friends to have peace.

Answered Prayer

Again I say to you, that if two of you agree on earth about anything that they may ask, it shall be done for them by My Father who is in heaven. MATTHEW *18:18*

As Sara wrote about world peace, she had heard about an answer to the prayers of many faithful Christians on the other side of the world. The news announced that the Mawozo gang suddenly released the last of seventeen Christian missionaries kidnapped in Haiti. Fellow believers had fasted and prayed for two months, and, at last, believers everywhere rejoiced. What were the particular circumstances here? Why were they so filled with joy?

Late in the afternoon the next day, a convoy of a dozen vehicles, including US Embassy SUVs and Haitian police, transported the missionaries to the Port au Prince airport, and later they could be seen smiling and hugging each other.

A spokesman for the Christian organization had this to say one day after the crisis began: "As an organization, we commit this situation to God and trust Him to see us through. May the Lord Jesus be magnified, and may many more people come to know His love and salvation. We again want to affirm our commitment to trust God to guide us."

Sara reflected on his comments as the crisis began and then considered how God had graciously answered the prayers of many believers. She thanked God. Deep in her heart she knew this was only one of many traumatic situations going on in the world around her. Constant prayer

GROWING A PEACEFUL HEART

would be needed for God's intervention and direction in all corners of the globe.

For too long Sara had murmured within herself or rehashed world problems with others. Now, like the spokesman for the organization, she committed the situation to God. Sara prayed that she and others would trust Him in everything.

> **Today's Peace Step**
> Pray for relief from war, violence, and danger at home and around the world.

She asked for the Lord Jesus to be magnified and many more people come to know His love and salvation.

A Current Call

Be strong and take heart, all you who hope in the LORD.
PSALM *31:24 (NIV)*

After hearing about the Russian invasion of Ukraine, Ann could almost feel her face light up when she read about the Polish volunteers who were driving Ukrainian refugees to local train stations or directly to cities like Warsaw. Through online efforts or at airports and train stations, volunteers placed Ukrainians with families willing to host them in their own homes. Ann shook her head in amazement when she read that refugee numbers had reached over two million.

Soon Ann joined Christians around the world to pray for the Ukrainian people. She met with a group from her church that discussed the various means of helping and soon chose to donate money as her best way to help.

Ann later learned that people chose Psalm 31 as a global rallying cry for this situation. In this psalm David wrote of conspiracy and terror on every side, along with plots to take his own life. He then says, in verse 14–16, "But I trust in you, LORD; I say, 'You are my God.' My times are in your hands; deliver me from my enemies, from those who pursue me. Let your face shine on your servant; save me in your unfailing love" (NIV).

> **Today's Peace Step**
> Pray for people in turbulent times, and choose a tangible way to help.

Like Ann, you and I can pray for believers and unbelievers to seek and find their hope and peace in Jesus Christ and His gospel. This good news must soak its way through their hearts so that no leader or persecution can shake their faith. We can also pray that all believers will continue to find strength, comfort, and peace in God and share some of their strength and peace with others. We can, and should, lift up churches, missionaries, and individuals who are working to relieve pain and to provide lodging and love as needed.

Peace Today (Biblical Story)

Peace I leave with you; my peace I give you. I do not give to you as the world gives. Do not let your hearts be troubled and do not be afraid. JOHN 14:27 (NIV)

Shortly before his arrest and crucifixion, Jesus told his disciples they would all soon desert Him. They didn't believe Him, but they ran off when the trouble started. Peter denied Jesus three times as predicted by Jesus.

Rather than turn on His followers, Jesus offered words of hope. He reminded them that in the world they would have trouble. But He assured them that He had overcome the world (John 16:33). Where is the peace? "In me," Christ said. Where is the trouble? In this world, Christ indicated.

Jesus shared about eternal life and promised to send the Holy Spirit. Today's verse reminds us that Jesus gives us peace while we are here on earth. We just need to let go of worry and fear. He quietly stood trial and let soldiers beat Him and place a crown of thorns on His head. He carried a cross and let soldiers hammer nails through His feet and hands. He suffered. He did it for us, so we might believe His words and have the peace He spoke about. He showed us peace as He suffered. When you look at a cross, remember what Jesus did.

> **Today's Peace Step**
> Pray this Scripture: "Do not be anxious about anything, but in every situation, by prayer and petition, with thanksgiving, present your request to God. And the peace of God, which transcends all understanding, will guard your hearts and you minds in Christ Jesus" (Philippians 4:7, NIV).

Even as you stop at a traffic light that has crossroads, let the cross formed be a reminder of what Jesus did.

Jesus accepted the mission God the Father gave Him out of love.

A Profound Ministry (Historic Story)

And He said to them, "Go into all the world and preach the gospel to all creation." Mark 16:15

Place: Anywhere disasters occur.

Purpose: To proclaim the Gospel of Jesus Christ by every possible means and to equip the church and others to do the same, one on one or in large gatherings.

Privileges: Countless opportunities to offer physical, emotional, and spiritual support and relief around the world.

What is the organization's name? It's the Billy Graham Evangelical Association. It continues what Billy Graham started in his life on earth.

Founded in 1950, the organization continues to reach millions of people. They have served around the world in communities devastated by natural disasters, such as a tornado in Kentucky, a category four hurricane in Florida, and earthquakes in other countries. In Kentucky, Billy Graham's son, Franklin, and his wife, Jane, served meals to countless people who had lost their homes and loved ones, and their Rapid Response Team provided counseling to many in need. They are often the first organization on the ground that provides relief.

> **Today's Peace Step**
> Thank God for ministries that provide needed assistance, and volunteer to serve people in need.

Today the Billy Graham Evangelical Association also offers the Samaritan's Purse, which provides shoe boxes with gifts for needy children around the globe during Christmas as well as numerous other outreaches. Through their website, any individual may request information regarding their efforts around the world, spiritual encouragement, sermons, and Bible studies.

Billy Graham didn't start out to help in disaster relief. He started as a preacher in the 1940s, to share the gospel and help others know Jesus, the Prince of Peace. Many people responded, and his ministry grew. The growth included being a good neighbor to the world and helping those in need, especially the poor and those impacted by disasters.

How to Pray

It happened that while Jesus was praying in a certain place, when He had finished, one of His disciples said to Him, "Lord, teach us to pray, just as John also taught his disciples." LUKE 11:1

What is your greatest tool for peace and greatest power for change? It's prayer. What is your prayer life like? Is it based on the Word of God and the form of prayer Jesus gave His disciples in Matthew 6:9–11 and Luke 11:2–4? Maybe it will help to take a brief look at the Lord's Prayer.

The opening line is *Our Father who art in heaven.* As children run to their father for love, help, and mercy, so we must hurry to our heavenly Father in reverence and assurance.

The second line is *Hallowed by thy name.* We ask God to enable us and others to honor and glorify Him in all that we think, say, and do.

The third line is *Thy kingdom come.* We pray with confidence for Satan's kingdom to be abolished, for God's kingdom of grace to come through us and others, and for the kingdom of glory of Christ's return to come quickly.

The fourth line is *Thy will be done on earth as it is in heaven.* We ask God to help us accept His will and purpose for everyone on earth.

The fifth line is *Give us this day our daily bread.* Here we pray for God to meet our daily needs. We also recall that Jesus, the bread of life, is our spiritual food.

The sixth line is *And forgive us our debts, as we forgive our debtors.* For the sake of Christ, we pray for God to forgive our sins as we, by His grace, forgive others.

The seventh line is *And lead us not into temptation, but deliver us from evil.* We ask for God to keep us from Satan's temptation and to deliver us when temptation comes.

Today's Peace Step

Let this prayer be a model for how to pray and have peace when you pray.

The Lord's Prayer's conclusion comes from 1 Chronicles 29:11 and are not words Jesus spoke: *For thine is the kingdom, and the power, and the glory forever. Amen.* We are to find our encouragement from God alone and are to ascribe praise, power, and glory to Him for all our days. Finally, in our desire and assurance to be heard, we conclude with *Amen!*

CONTRIBUTING AUTHOR BIOS

Joan C. Benson (www.joancbenson.com) is a wife, mother, grandmother, author, and speaker. She has written for multiple Christian magazines and LifeWay's children's ministry. Her debut historical fiction novel, *His Gift*, was published by Elk Lake Publishing Inc. in 2020, and she has four children's books currently under contract.

Pam Farrel (www.Love-Wise.com) is an international speaker, relationship specialist, and author of fifty-six books including best-selling *Men Are Like Waffles, Women Are Like Spaghetti*. The Farrels are codirectors of Love-Wise Ministries. They enjoy time with their three sons, three daughters-in-law, and five grandchildren. They make their home on a live-aboard boat docked in Southern California.

Linda Gilden (www.lindagilden.com) is an award-winning writer, speaker, editor, and certified writing and speaking coach. Cofounder of the LINKED Personality

System, Linda helps others discover the peace of knowing who God created them to be. A mom and grandmother, she loves to float while reading a good book, surrounded by splashing grandchildren.

Linda Goldfarb (www.livepowerfullynow.org) is married to Sam and is the momma of four adult children and "Maw-Maw" to many grandchildren. She is also an award-winning author of the LINKED Personality series, an international speaker, the founder of Parenting Awesome Kids, and a board-certified, advanced-level Christian life coach specializing in personal and professional growth.

Amy L. Harden (www.AmyLHarden.com) is an author, speaker, wife, mother of five children, and Nanny to three granddaughters. She is a veteran Navy journalist, has written for *Guideposts* and Focus on the Family, and is presently working on her first novel. Connect with her on her website or on Facebook and Instagram.

Award-winning author **Melissa Henderson** (http://www.melissaghenderson.com) writes inspirational messages sometimes laced with a bit of humor. With stories in books, magazines, devotionals, and articles, Melissa hopes to encourage readers. Her family motto is "It's Always a Story with The Hendersons." Follow Melissa on her website and on social media.

Britt Mooney (www.brittmooney.com) believes great stories change the world and coffee fuels the adventure. He is the author of *Say Yes: How God-Sized Dreams Take Flight* that details how Phoenix Roasters, a missional coffee company raised money for world missions. He's also a church planter, and coffee marketer from Suwanee, GA with his wife, Becca, and 3 kids.

Joan Patterson (www.joanpatterson.org) is an author and speaker. She enjoys demonstrating the exceptional skills of Giles, her service dog. Joan has a degree in business and education from Liberty University. Her articles have appeared in various magazines. She lives in York, Pennsylvania, with Giles and her husband of fifty-one years.

PeggySue Wells (www.PeggySueWells.com) is the solo mom of seven, founder of SingleMomCircle.com, and bestselling author of thirty books including *The Ten Best Decisions A Single Mom Can Make.*